Resolving
Conflicts

Resolving Conflicts

INTERACTIVE DISCOVERY BOOK
DEVOTIONAL AND JOURNAL

JOSH MCDOWELL

AND

ED STEWART

WORD PUBLISHING

NASHVILLE

A Thomas Nelson Company

Scripture quotations used in this book are from the Holy Bible, New International Version. Copyright © 1973, 1978, 1984, International Bible Society. Used by permission of Zondervan Bible Publishers.

Other Scripture references are from the following sources:

The Holy Bible, New Living Translation (NLT), copyright © 1996. Used by permission of Tyndale House Publishers, Inc., Wheaton, Illinois. All rights reserved. New American Standard Bible (NASB), © 1960, 1977 by the Lockman Foundation.

Library of Congress Cataloging-in-Publication Data

McDowell, Josh.
    Handling conflicts : interactive discovery book : devotional and journal for youth / by Josh McDowell and Ed Stewart.
      p. cm.
    ISBN 0-8499-3788-4 (pbk.)
    1. Youth—Religious life. 2. Conflict management—Religious aspects—Christianity. 3. Parent and child—Religious aspects—Christianity. 4. Youth—Prayer-books and devotions—English. I. Stewart, Ed II. Title.

BV4597.53.C58 M36 2000
248.8'3—dc21

00-024464
CIP

Printed in the United States of America

00 01 02 03 04 05 PC 9 8 7 6 5 4 3 2 1

Resolving Conflicts

KEN'S STORY

When his dad walked into his room, fifteen-year-old Ken Meyers knew what he would say. This conversation happened at least once a week during the school year, sometimes twice.

"I thought you had homework to do," Dad said, lifting the headphones from Ken's ears and placing them on the bedside table. Ken bristled inside. He felt like a little kid when his dad just took things away from him like that.

Ken, who had been lying on his bed listening to music, sat up. "I *do* have homework," Ken said, displaying the language-arts worksheet in his hand, "and I'm doing it." He was about halfway through an exercise of diagramming sentences and identifying parts of speech.

"You know you will concentrate better without that noise rattling your brain." Dad motioned toward the headphones, which were jacked into Ken's portable CD player. The music was still playing, but it was faint and tinny coming from the tiny headphone speakers on the table.

"It's not noise, Dad, it's music—*Christian* music," Ken said respectfully. He hated the frequent lectures, but it only got worse if he let his attitude get the best of him.

Dad's hands went to his hips, his classic lecture pose. "That is not music, Kenneth. It sounds like a bunch of spoons caught in the garbage disposal. And there is no way ruckus like that can be called Christian. Just because a group says it is Christian doesn't mean its message is coming from God."

Ken wanted to argue the point. *Listen to the words, Dad. They are just as biblical as any of those cassettes of hymns you and Mom play. As for the music, it's a "joyful sound." You're so paranoid that I may be listening to satanic music.* But he had tried that approach before, and the lecture had only lasted longer. So Ken kept his thoughts to himself.

"Besides, I could never do homework with the TV or radio on," his dad continued. "It ruins your concentration."

It may ruin your *concentration, Dad, but it doesn't ruin mine. The music actually keeps me relaxed and helps me concentrate. Can't you accept that my study habits may be different from yours?* Ken felt the anger steaming up inside him, but he kept silent.

"You can't afford to waste study time, Kenneth. Your grades are slipping. You're barely pulling Bs and Cs. This is not middle school, Son. You have to bear down if you want to achieve the grades that will get you into State University."

I've tried to tell you that I don't want to go to State, Dad, Ken argued silently. *In fact, I don't think I want to go to any college right after high school. I want to take at least a year off to travel with a Christian band or take a short-term missions trip. Maybe then I'll know what I want to do with my life. If you would only listen to me sometimes, you might understand what's going on in my life. But all you can think about are my grades.*

"And what about these?" his dad pressed. The man's hand left his hip long enough to point to the shoe box on the bed next to Ken.

2

"Those are my baseball cards."

"I can see that they are baseball cards, Kenneth," his dad snapped. "I mean, what are they doing here beside you while you are studying?"

"I don't study every single minute, Dad," Ken snapped back. "I keep them here so I can look at them when I need a break."

"It's just another temptation to waste time," his dad said firmly. Then he reached out as if to take the box away.

Ken grabbed the box, ready to pull it back. "It's my hobby, Dad," he argued. "Don't worry, I'm not going to fail English because I look at a few cards now and then." Ken had allowed his sarcasm to come out a little too strongly, and he wished he could take it back. He never won when he fought with his dad.

For a moment Ken and his father eyed each other without speaking, each with a hand on the box of baseball cards. "I'm going to put these cards away so they won't distract you," Dad said, starting to pull from his end of the box.

Common sense told Ken to let go of the box and drop the argument. But he was too mad to listen to his better judgment. "They're not distracting me, Dad. I can study just as well with—"

Ken's end of the box tore open in the subtle tug-of-war and more than 300 baseball cards spilled onto the bed and the floor. His dad was left holding the torn and suddenly empty shoe box. Ken wished he hadn't been so bullheaded, but he was tired of caving in when his parents tried to mold him into their idea of a student. He had never resisted his father like this before, and he was a little afraid of the possible consequences.

Dad studied the mess of cards for a moment, then glared at his son. Ken was afraid that his collection of baseball cards was history. Instead, Dad dropped the box to the floor and scooped up the CD player and carry-case of CDs from the bedside table. "I don't want to see these again, Kenneth," he announced, shaking his finger at the mess of cards, "and you won't be listening to this so-called music until your GPA comes up a full point." Then he left the room, closing the door behind him.

Ken was so angry he almost cried. If it wasn't his grades or music Dad and Mom disapproved of, it was his clothes or his hairstyle or his friends. His baseball card collection was "frivolous," they said. (He should get into biking or rock climbing, something that gave him exercise.) When Ken tried to explain his preferences, they didn't seem to listen. And when he wanted to show off his latest card or Christian CD, his mom and dad were not interested. Ken didn't know which bothered him more: their active disapproval or their passive disinterest.

Losing his CD player and "tunes" was pretty bad. But Ken was relieved that his dad had not also confiscated the baseball card collection. Nor had Dad ordered him to get rid of them; he'd only said that he didn't want to see them again. Pulling another sturdy athletic shoe box from his closet, he began gathering his cards and angrily stacking them inside. He would keep his cards hidden when Dad was at home and pull them out only when he was away. It made him feel like a hunted spy in his own home. And the fact that his father had ripped off his music made him feel like a prisoner.

Just before 10:00 P.M., Ken climbed into bed for the night. He had not finished his homework. Tonight's clash with his dad had sapped him of the little motivation he'd had. He knew another incomplete assignment would pull down his grades even further. But what difference did it make? Even if he notched a 4.0 for the semester, his parents would continue to chip away at his other differences and failures. For all his trying, he couldn't seem to win with them. So why try?

Dad and Mom were in the family room watching TV as usual, so Ken knew they would not notice that his light was out. They seldom talked to him at bedtime anymore. No way did Ken want to return to his younger years when Dad or Mom tucked him in each night, read stories, said prayers, and smothered him with kisses. That was OK for his younger sister, Hillary, but way too much for him. Yet no contact at bedtime didn't feel right either. It seemed that the only time his parents spoke to him was to criticize him or correct him, and the only time they touched him was to push his feet off the sofa.

Lying in the darkness, Ken lifted a silent prayer. *God, I know You love me, but I'm not so sure Dad and Mom do. Why do they seem to be against everything I do? Why don't they care about my life, my feelings, my ideas, and my interests? I know some things I do really tick them off. But they seem to disapprove of everything. It's like they're tired of being my parents and wish I would just grow up and move out. Why can't I get along with them, God?*

As he prayed, it occurred to Ken that home wasn't the only place where his relationships were wearing thin. The face of Todd Wallace, his friend at church, suddenly popped into his mind. *Yeah, some friend*, Ken thought cynically. *Todd is great to be around when we're doing what he wants to do. But when I ask him to go the sports card shop with me, or if I need his help on a youth group outreach event, he is suddenly "too busy." It's like he's my friend when I fit in with his plans or when he needs something. Otherwise he could care less.*

Ken quickly added a postscript to his prayer. *And, God, why can't Todd and I be real friends?*

Just before drifting off to sleep, Ken thought about Doug Shaw. Doug and his wife, Jenny, were volunteer youth leaders at the church his family attended. A couple of years earlier, Doug had helped Ken make the transition from getting by on his parents' faith to trusting Christ personally for himself. Ken loved the youth group at church, and he considered Doug his spiritual big brother. Doug Shaw frequently told kids in the group that he and Jenny were available to talk with them about anything. For the first time since he had met Doug, Ken realized he had something he really wanted to talk about.

After school the next day, Ken walked to the small downtown quick-print shop Doug and Jenny owned and operated. The shop was not exactly on Ken's way home, but he walked the extra six blocks anyway, hoping Doug was there and hoping he'd have a minute to talk.

Walking into the shop, Ken felt a little odd. He had never done this before. Should he have made an appointment? What was he supposed to say? "Hey Doug, I have a problem. Will you stop working and solve it for me?" didn't sound too good. As it turned out, Ken didn't have to worry about it. Doug, who was doing layout on one of the shop's computers, saw him come in the door.

"Hi, Ken," he said cheerfully. "What a nice surprise to have you drop in."

Jenny, who was waiting on a customer at the counter, also waved and smiled. Ken waved back. "Give me a couple of minutes, Ken," Doug called over the counter, "and I'll take a break. There's something I want to tell you. We can get something to drink."

"Sure," Ken said, nodding. Doug made him feel like a welcomed guest instead of an interruption in his schedule. It was a feeling he had been missing at home, where he sometimes felt like an intruder or a pest.

Five minutes later Doug and Ken left the shop in Jenny's care and headed down the sidewalk toward a place called The Blender. As they walked, Doug grabbed Ken by the shoulder and gave it a gentle squeeze. "I want to thank you for helping out with the sound during our youth outreach event last weekend," Doug said. "I saw you toting mike cords and speakers all over the place, and I appreciate your help."

Ken enjoyed getting caught doing something good for a change. He had worked hard with the sound crew during the big event, and he didn't think anybody had noticed.

"I enjoyed it," he said. "I'd like to work with sound again sometime."

They each bought a cold fruit smoothie then sat down together in a booth. They talked about the great music and dynamic speaker at the youth outreach event and the number of students who had trusted Christ as their Savior that night. Ken knew Doug had to get back to the shop soon. It would have been easy to skip the real reason he had come to see Doug. But he was afraid things would get much worse at home if he didn't talk to someone soon.

"I have kind of a prayer request to talk to you about, if you don't mind," Ken said, fiddling with the straw in his drink.

"I don't mind at all, Ken," Doug assured. "What can I pray with you about?"

Ken had told no one but God what he was about to reveal to Doug. The thought of actually telling another person about the anger and hurt he felt toward his parents and his friend Todd made him pause to swallow a surprising lump of emotion that had suddenly crept into his throat. "I'm . . . I'm having trouble with my parents. We're not getting along very well right now." He briefly described the latest clash with his dad over the baseball cards. "It seems that everything I do is stupid or wrong. They're always ragging on me about my clothes or my music or my grades. They don't seem to care about who I am and what I like. Sometimes I feel like I'm living in the house alone. I don't know if they really love me." When he finished his explanation, Ken had tears in his eyes.

Doug's face clouded with sorrow. "Ken, I can see that this really hurts you. I'm sorry you are experiencing doubt about your parents' love. Seeing you in pain makes my heart hurt for you."

Ken felt some of the weight lift from him. Just knowing that Doug understood where he was coming from and hurt for him was a measure of relief he had not expected. Feeling his confidence swell, Ken went on to tell Doug about his recent difficulties in getting along with Todd Wallace.

After a few respectful moments, Doug said, "Tell me more about your relationship with your parents."

"What do you want to know?"

"How would you describe your relationship with your dad?"

Ken pulled the straw out of his drink and watched the juice drip into the glass. "If we're not talking about me—like what's wrong with what I'm doing and stuff—we usually don't talk. He's busy with his work and his hobbies."

"Does your dad ever have time for you?"

Ken shook his head slowly. "No."

"Do you feel like nothing you do is good enough for him?"

"*Nothing* I do is ever good enough for him," Ken emphasized, rubbing the hint of a small tear from his eye.

Doug asked several more questions about Ken's relationship with his parents. Then he gently probed into Ken's friendship with Todd. Each sad answer was accompanied by a shadow of sorrow on his face.

Finally Doug said, "I have to get back to the shop. But maybe we can get together again soon so we can talk more about the conflicts in your relationships and pray together. Would that be OK?"

"Yeah, that would be OK."

Since they both attended the 9:30 A.M. worship service on Sundays, they decided to meet at church during the 11:00 service. Doug said he knew about an empty Sunday school classroom they could use then. Ken eagerly agreed.

"Until then," Doug said, "I want you to know that I care about you, Ken. I know it hurts to feel that your parents don't understand you and that Todd is so self-centered in his friendship toward you. I want to stay with you through this. I'll be praying for you. In fact, let me say a prayer for you right now." Ken fought back another tear as Doug quietly asked God to share His comfort with Ken.

When Doug said good-bye and returned to the shop, Ken was not eager to go home. He knew he would probably be quizzed and criticized for getting home late. And he sure couldn't tell Todd about his talk with Doug. But he felt a spark of comfort and encouragement knowing that he was not alone in his pain. Doug knew and Doug cared, and that meant a lot to Ken. It gave him a glimmer of hope that someday his relationships with three important people in his life might get better.

TIME OUT TO CONSIDER

Is your relationship with your parents anything like Ken's? Do you seem to be at odds with them about practically everything? Do you hear far more criticisms at home than compliments? Do your mom and/or dad give you grief about your appearance, your manners (or lack of them), your room, your music, your friends, your grades, or your activities? Do they easily catch you doing things wrong and hardly ever notice when you do things right? Do many of your conversations end up as arguments or shouting matches? Does it seem that they are more interested in your brothers or sisters than in you? Do you sometimes wonder if your parents really love you?

In some families, parent-child conflicts may be so severe that they can be described as abusive. Some parents neglect their children's basic needs for shelter, food, clothing, medical attention, education, and so on. Arguments deteriorate into physical attacks or vicious name calling. Children in these kinds of homes should report physical, sexual, or emotional abuse to the proper authorities because of imminent danger to their life and health.

Yet in many homes, like Ken's, parents are not criminally negligent or abusive. In fact, Ken's Christian parents provide well for his basic needs, and they do not abuse their children physically or sexually. However, they may be guilty of being inattentive to many of Ken's less obvious emotional needs. This may be the case in your family. Your parents may provide a fairly safe, healthy environment in which to live and generally care for your physical well-being. But you may struggle to get along because they don't seem to understand that you need more than three meals a day and a roof over your head to feel loved and accepted.

And how about the other important relationships in your life? Are any of them like Ken's "friendship" with Todd? Are you on great terms with somebody one week and then seemingly strangers or enemies the next because of conflicts? Whether you are clashing with your parents, your friends, or other people, the issue is basically the same. You have valid emotional needs, and when those needs are ignored, conflicts arise.

If this describes some of your relationships, it is important that you understand three things. First, it will be helpful for you to know *why* people are inattentive to some of your needs. Second, you must identify the specific needs in your life that are being overlooked or ignored by others. Third, it is important to understand how to talk to your parents and others about your needs. This booklet will help you in all three areas.

First, let's talk about why your parents may be unaware of your needs. Parenting is a tough job, and there are no perfect parents. Adults must juggle many demands of life in addition to raising their children. With the pressures and responsibilities of marriage, career, finances, and outside activities, many parents find it difficult to give their full attention and care to their children. There are a variety of reasons why parents may be inattentive to the needs of their children. Perhaps your parents are struggling with one or more of the following.

Financial pressure. Many parents work so hard each week to put food on the table and pay the bills that their children are sometimes neglected. Some single parents must work two jobs to make ends meet, leaving little time for the children. In many two-parent homes, both Dad and Mom work full time. Financial pressures can be so exhausting that parents have little attention or energy left for their children.

Hectic lifestyle. Parents are often so involved with the demands

10

of a busy life that some important things are left undone. Career, church, and community activities may keep them going day and night. And the activities of their children—sports, school functions, music lessons, camps, church activities, and more—just add to their hectic schedules. Parents may be so busy *doing* things for and with their children that they overlook the important role of just *being* attentive parents.

Family breakup. Divorce and single parenting create great stress on parents. One parent may be left with the parenting work of two. Extra financial burdens, the beginning of a new career or education track, and new relationships may distract the parent and make careful attention to each child seemingly impossible.

Large families. The more children there are in the family, the harder it may be to give appropriate attention and care to each.

Self-centeredness. Parents tend to neglect their children if they are constantly preoccupied with their own interests and activities. The drive to climb the social ladder or achieve status and wealth is sometimes elevated above the emotional needs of the children.

Lack of parenting skills. Some parents just don't know how to meet all the needs of their children. They mistakenly believe that parenting only means providing for the physical and material needs of their children.

It is highly unlikely that your parents are purposely inattentive to your needs or disagreeable toward you and your lifestyle. Are one or more of the reasons listed above keeping them from meeting some of your needs?

Similar characteristics are likely at the root of your conflicts with friends and others. Mainly, your friends are sometimes clueless about your emotional needs because they are too busy with their own lives, because they are too self-centered, or because they lack the sensitivity and skills for being a caring, supportive friend.

Ken's concern over his relational conflicts have negatively affected his grades. His motivation and concentration have been dulled by a lack of encouragement and interest from his parents. How have your difficulties at home impacted your daily life? There are many negative effects that result when people don't get along. Perhaps you will identify with one or more of the following:

- You may feel that you are unimportant or worthless.

- Like Ken, your concentration and motivation in school may be weak, and your grades may suffer as a result.

- Lacking full acceptance from the people you care about, you may be tempted to hang out with others who negatively influence your moral and spiritual values.

- You may have difficulty finding and developing other good relationships.

- You may be tempted to rebel against your parents or hurt your friends in order to gain their attention or to punish them for their lack of attentiveness.

- Lack of close interaction or caring in relationships may tempt you to get involved with alcohol or drugs.

- You may be tempted to find the intimacy you miss in sexual activity.

How are you dealing with your struggle to get along with others and the negative effects of this conflict in your life? Ken Meyers demonstrated a good example of how to respond. He went to a trusted Christian friend and mentor, Doug Shaw, and told him about his problems. You may experience a wide range of feelings about your conflicts. You may feel sad, depressed, hopeless, abandoned, frightened, and even angry. You may cry about what is happening. You may feel emotionally drained. Or you may get angry at the situation, at your parents or friends, or even at God for allowing it to happen.

It is important to understand that all these feelings are normal and natural. It is the way God wired you. Your emotions are a built-in release valve to help you handle the inner pain. Of course, there are both productive and unproductive ways of expressing these emotions.

When Ken went to Doug and poured out his story and hurt, he was taking the first healthy step in dealing with his situation. This response reflects Jesus' words in Matthew 5:4: "Blessed are those who mourn, for they will be comforted." Mourning is the process of getting the hurt out. You vulnerably share how you feel so others can feel your pain with you. This is God's design for blessing you and beginning to heal the pain that accompanies a difficult struggle in your relationships. It is good and necessary that you experience the different emotions that come at this time.

Your greatest need as you express your pain is for others to comfort you. That's what Doug was doing as Ken told his story, feeling Ken's pain and sharing the sorrow with him. In a time of emotional hurt, our greatest comfort comes when others sorrow with us. One major way God shares His comfort with us is through other people. The apostle Paul wrote, "God . . . comforts us in all our troubles, so that we can comfort those in any trouble with the comfort we ourselves have received from God" (2 Cor. 1:3–4).

What is comfort? Maybe it will help to first see what comfort is *not*. Comfort is not a "pep talk" urging you to hang in there, tough it out, or hold it together. Comfort is not an attempt to explain why bad things happen to people. Comfort is not a bunch of positive words about God being in control and everything being OK. All of these things may be good and useful in time, but they do not fill our primary need for comfort.

People comfort us primarily by feeling our hurt and sorrowing with us. Jesus illustrated the ministry of comfort when His friend Lazarus died (see John 11). When Jesus arrived at the home of Lazarus's sisters, Mary and Martha, He wept with them (see vv.

33–35). His response is especially interesting in light of what He did next: raise Lazarus from the dead (see vv. 38–44).

Why didn't Jesus simply tell the grieving Mary and Martha, "No need to cry, my friends, because in a few minutes Lazarus will be alive again"? Because at that moment they needed someone to cry with them. Jesus met Mary and Martha's need for comfort by sharing in their sorrow and tears. Later He performed the miracle that turned their sorrow to joy.

We receive comfort when we know we are not suffering alone. Paul instructed us, "Rejoice with those who rejoice; mourn with those who mourn" (Rom. 12:15). When you experience sorrow, people may try to comfort you by cheering you up, urging you to be strong, or trying to explain away the tragic event. These people no doubt care about you and mean well by their words. But, hopefully, there is also someone around like Doug Shaw who will provide the comfort you need. You will sense God's care and concern for you as this someone hurts with you, sorrows with you, and even weeps with you. Doug Shaw is a good example of what real comfort looks like in painful circumstances.

So your first response to your struggle is to share your burden with someone who cares about you. It may be a youth leader like Doug Shaw, your minister, or a mature, trusted Christian friend. But there is more to dealing with your situation than pouring out your story and receiving comfort, as Ken Meyers is about to find out.

KEN'S STORY

Ken's mind often wandered during sermons, but it was especially difficult to pay attention today. Sitting with his parents and his sister, Hillary, in the sanctuary, Ken considered the irony. To others in the church, the Meyerses probably looked like the ideal Christian family. But to Ken, this didn't feel like a family at all. His parents seemed more like jailers, restricting his privileges and general enjoyment of life until he had served his "sentence" and earned his freedom at age eighteen. Ken wondered if anything Doug Shaw could say would make a difference in his relationship with his dad and mom. He had similar doubts about his once good friend Todd.

A little after 11:00, Ken met Doug in an empty Sunday school classroom. Ken had not told his parents *why* he was meeting with Doug, only that Doug wanted to talk to him. Dad and Mom had eagerly given permission for Ken to stay, saying they would pick him up in front of the church at noon. *They probably hope Doug will talk some sense into me about my "worldly" behavior,* he thought cynically.

"How's it been going at home since we talked last week, Ken?" Doug began.

Ken shrugged. "About the same, I guess. It's like I'm not even part of the family. I live there and sleep there, but Dad and Mom don't notice me unless I do something they don't approve of—and they seem to find plenty of those things each week."

"I'm sad that you don't feel as close to your parents as you want to," Doug said. "I've been praying for you since we talked at The Blender because I really care about you."

Ken dropped his head sheepishly. "Thanks." Doug's prayers and concern meant more to him than he could express. "And thanks for the note you sent to me. It really helped."

"Let me ask you a question, Ken," Doug continued. "It will help us get into your struggles with your parents. And it will lead us to some guidelines that should help you at home and with your friend Todd."

Ken nodded. "OK, shoot."

"Have you ever said something like this at home: 'Hey, Mom and Dad, I'm getting hungry. What's for dinner?'"

Ken raised an eyebrow, wondering where Doug was going with his question. "Of course, like about five times a week. What do you mean by—"

Doug cut him off with his next question. "And do your parents always provide dinner and other meals for you?"

"Yeah, of course," Ken said, still wondering what food had to do with his problem. "And if they aren't around at mealtime, there is always something in the fridge I can nuke. Why do you ask?"

"Let me ask one more question, then I think you will understand," Doug said. "Have you ever said to your mom or dad, 'I'm really feeling ignored. Do you have fifteen minutes you can spend with me?'"

Ken studied Doug's expression, which conveyed that he had a secret he was just bursting to tell. "No way," Ken answered finally. "I mean, can you imagine any kid like me saying that to his parents? It never happens."

Doug pressed on. "But when you're hungry, you're not afraid to ask them for something to eat, right?"

"Right."

"Then why can't you express your other needs and respectfully ask your parents to meet them?"

Ken didn't answer because he didn't know what to say. He had never considered telling his parents what he really felt.

Apparently Doug wasn't expecting an answer because he kept talking, "From what you have told me, Ken, your relationship with your parents would probably improve if they just sat down and listened to you occasionally and showed a little interest in some of your activities."

Ken smiled at the incredible thought. "It sure couldn't hurt."

"And how would you feel if they started to notice your positive behavior and complimenting you when you did something right?"

Ken gave a small laugh. "I'd feel like they were on drugs."

Doug grinned at the humor. Then he said, "Seriously, if your parents began treating you this way, would your relationship with them better meet your expectations? Would you sense that they love you?"

Ken didn't hesitate. "Of course, but—"

Doug interrupted him by holding up his hand like a stop sign.

"How will your parents understand how you want to be treated unless you tell them?" He didn't wait for an answer. "You have certain emotional needs, Ken—everybody does. You tell Mom and Dad about your physical hunger for food, and they fill that need. I believe if you tell them about your emotional hunger for attention and approval, they will try to meet those needs too, because I think they really do love you."

Ken felt a mild flash of panic. "What do you mean by 'tell them'?"

"I mean 'tell them,'" Doug explained with an impish smile. "Sit down with your parents, explain your needs, and respectfully ask for their help in meeting them. Try the same thing with Todd. You need to tell him what you feel you need out of your relationship."

Ken was on his feet and pacing. "I don't know if I can do that with my parents," he said nervously.

"Sure you can," Doug said, sounding rock-solid confident. "I'll even go with you if you want."

Ken stopped pacing. "You'll talk to my parents for me?"

"I'll talk to your parents *with* you," Doug corrected, "after you and I have talked and prayed together about your specific needs and how they are not being met."

Ken could hardly believe it. "You would really do this?"

"Only if you want me to," Doug said. "And once we have gone through the process with your parents, you will know how to talk to Todd."

"That would be great," Ken said, dropping back into his chair with a relieved sigh.

During the next forty minutes, Doug helped Ken think through and list on paper specific areas where his relationship with his parents was strained. The discussion helped them to identify three of Ken's emotional needs that were not being met at home. Then they prayed together that God would prepare the way for a positive, productive meeting with Ken's parents. Finally,

Doug suggested that they repeat the process after Ken cleared the air with his mom and dad.

When Ken's dad arrived to pick him up, Doug asked if he could stop by later in the afternoon for a visit. "Ken and I have something we want to share with you," he said cordially.

Mr. Meyers agreed.

Ken rode home in silence, already nervous about the meeting, but also expectant that something good was about to happen between him and his mom and dad.

TIME OUT TO CONSIDER

Ken needed more than the comfort of his youth leader to get through the conflict with his parents and friend, and so do you. There are two more important elements that hopefully are being supplied to you.

First, you need the support of others. What's the difference between comfort and support? People supply the comfort you need when they share your sorrow emotionally. People supply the support you need by helping you in practical, useful ways. You need the help of people who are committed to obeying Galatians 6:2: "Carry each other's burdens, and in this way you will fulfill the law of Christ."

Think about how Doug Shaw supported Ken. In addition to being a source of comfort, Doug helped Ken think through the practical steps of identifying unmet emotional needs and then committed to meet with Ken's parents. It is one thing to have someone there to share your pain and sorrow in a conflict. It is something else to have one or more persons step in and help you resolve the conflict.

You may be tempted to ignore or refuse the support offered by others. You may feel like you can handle it yourself, or you may not want to bother other people with your problems. Resist that temptation. God put Galatians 6:2 in the Bible because He knows there are times we should rely on the support of others. This is such a time. Let other people help you, and be grateful for their help. It is one of the ways God is providing for you at this time.

What if you need practical help and nobody steps up to offer it? Ask for it. There is nothing wrong with telling a trusted friend, a youth leader, or your minister about your need and asking for help. In most cases, people are more than willing to help out; they just don't know what needs to be done. Feel free to help people support you at this time by letting them know what you need.

Second, you need the encouragement of others. You receive encouragement when someone does something thoughtful to lift your spirits. Ken was encouraged by Doug's commitment to pray for him. He was encouraged by the affirming words Doug shared in writing and whenever they spoke. And he was encouraged by Doug's willingness to work through the practical aspects of his conflict at home. Encouraging deeds like these may not seem as practical as solving problems, but they are just as necessary.

Once again, if you do not receive the encouragement you need, ask for it. It's OK to tell someone who cares about you, "I need a hug" or "I just need you to be with me for a while."

As Ken discovered, there are practical steps you can take to resolve your difficulties with others. When you don't get along with people, you may think that they are just being difficult and unreasonable. This may be partly true, but there is often a deeper issue. As Doug pointed out to Ken, the conflict may exist because some of your needs are not being met. Everyone has needs. We have physical needs for food, rest, and safety. We have spiritual needs for forgiveness, fellowship with God, and freedom from guilt and shame. And we have emotional needs, such as the need for love, security, and a sense of belonging.

Do not be ashamed or embarrassed about being needy; God has created us with these needs and provided the means for getting them met. Philippians 4:19 reads, "My God will meet all your needs according to his glorious riches in Christ Jesus." This verse reveals three clear facts: (1) God knows you have needs; (2) God wants to meet your needs; (3) God can meet your needs according to His glorious riches in Christ.

God meets some of your needs directly through His relationship with you. He is ultimately the source of all fulfilled needs, and He wants to see all your needs met. But He has chosen to meet a large number of your needs through your relationships with others. At this point in your life, your relationship with your parents is His primary avenue for meeting many of your emotional needs. He may also use other family members, church leaders, and your friends to meet some of your needs. But your parents are the key instruments God uses for meeting your needs, including emotional needs.

What are your emotional needs? Like Ken, you may not know how to answer that question. And it is possible that your parents and friends are not meeting some of your emotional needs because they have not identified them either. But just imagine what could happen in your relationships if you could identify some of your needs, share them with your parents, and begin to work with Dad and Mom—instead of against them—to see those needs met. And think how that same process could help clear up conflicts between you and some of your friends.

Six common emotional needs often go unmet in relationships. They are the need for attention, appreciation, approval, acceptance, respect, and affection. God created us with these needs, and He gave us parents and others to help meet them. Conflicts between people often arise when these needs are neither identified nor communicated. Like Doug said, you tell your parents when you feel hungry and in need of food. Why not tell them when you are needy emotionally so they can better meet those needs?

As you read about these six needs, two or three of them may stand out to you. They are likely your most pressing emotional needs at this time. At some point in the future, it will be helpful for you to talk to your parents about them.

Attention. Our need for attention is met when someone enters our world by showing interest and concern for who we are and what we do. If any of the following statements are true of you, perhaps your need for attention is not being fully met in your closest relationships.

- My parents or friends don't ever listen to me.

- My parents or friends don't have time for me.

- I often feel ignored by my parents or friends.

- Dad and Mom rarely do anything with me.

- My friends never want to do what I want to do.

- My parents almost never come to anything I'm involved in (concerts, ball games, etc.).

Appreciation. We feel appreciated when others share words of gratitude or praise for what we do. If you can identify with any of these statements, your need for appreciation is not being fully met.

- My parents seldom notice when I do something around the house.

- Mom and Dad talk about my bad behavior, but hardly ever mention the good things.

- I don't think my parents or friends are aware of my positive qualities.

- I hardly ever hear the words "Thank you" from my parents or friends.

Approval. Our need for approval is met when others compliment our deeds and speak well of us. These statements reflect a student whose need for approval is not being met by his or her parents or friends. Are they true of you?

- Nothing I do is good enough for my parents or friends.
- I feel like my parents or friends don't approve of me.
- It seems that my parents or friends criticize me all the time.
- My parents or friends sometimes make me feel like a complete failure.

Acceptance. We feel accepted when people know we are different and imperfect and love us anyway. Someone who doesn't feel accepted may make these statements.

- My parents or friends only seem to care about me if I do what they want me to do.
- Dad and Mom can't accept the fact that I'm different from them.
- Sometimes I feel like I don't really belong in this family.
- My parents or friends treat me like I don't know anything.
- When I mess up, my parents or friends can't seem to forgive me.

Respect. Our need for respect is met when we feel highly valued and esteemed by others. You may identify with the following statements if you don't feel respected by your parents.

- I feel like my parents or friends are always yelling at me.
- I don't have any privacy at home.
- I feel like my parents or friends don't trust me.
- Mom and Dad treat me like a little kid.
- My parents are always checking up on me.

Affection. Affection is communicated through physical closeness and loving words. A lack of parent-to-child affection is reflected in the following statements.

- It seems that my parents treat my brother/sister better than they treat me.
- I wish I felt closer to my parents or friends.
- My parents hardly ever tell me they love me.
- Dad and Mom seldom hug me or kiss me anymore.
- I don't receive much affection from my parents or friends.
- I know my parents love me, but sometimes they don't act like it.

Which are your two or three greatest unmet needs among these six? Prayerfully and respectfully share these needs with your parents and friends and see how you can work together to get your needs met.

At the same time, you must remember that meeting needs in relationships is a two-way street. Your parents and friends also have needs for attention, appreciation, approval, acceptance, respect, and affection. You should not feel that you are the primary source for meeting these needs. But there may be ways you can help meet these needs, further improving your relationships.

How do you approach your parents or friends to share your needs with them? Ken Meyers is about to find out, with the help of his youth leader and friend Doug Shaw.

KEN'S STORY

"Mom and Dad, I've been talking to Doug recently, and he has really helped me see some things in my life more clearly." Ken was so nervous that his voice squeaked when he spoke. He couldn't help it. It was late Sunday afternoon, and he was seated with his parents in the family room of their home. Doug Shaw was sitting nearby. Ken's younger sister, Hillary, was at a friend's house for the afternoon.

Ken went on. "As we talked, I came to better appreciate how well you take care of me. I mean, you provide a nice, safe home and plenty to eat. You buy most of my clothes and stuff for me. I just want you to know that I'm thankful for all you do. I know I don't tell you that enough." Ken swallowed hard. "And I . . . I love you both."

He noticed a glimmer of a smile on their faces. "We love you too, Kenneth," his mom said. Dad nodded.

Ken cleared his throat. He found it very difficult to say these words, and he wished he could leave the room and let Doug do the talking for him. But he knew he had to go on.

"Since you are so good at taking care of my needs, we—er, I mean, I—want to tell you about a couple of other areas where I kind of need your help. Would that be OK?"

"Of course, Ken," Dad said, and both his parents waited expectantly.

Ken squirmed uncomfortably in his seat, glanced at Doug for encouragement, then began. "Well, I'm learning that I have a pretty big need for your approval. I know I screw up a lot, and you tell me about it when I do. I need to be corrected sometimes. But it would help me if you'd also mention when I do something right. I just need to hear that you approve of me in some areas. When I don't hear your approval, I begin to think everything I do is wrong. If either of you notices something I do right, would you be willing to tell me about it?"

Ken was too nervous to look his parents in the eye. He stole a glance at Doug, who flashed him a "good job" smile. Then he waited.

After several silent seconds, his dad said, "Do you really think we don't approve of you?"

"Sometimes, Dad, especially when I only hear that my grades aren't good enough, that you don't like my clothes, that my room is always messy . . . " Ken could have added more to the list, but he didn't want to overdo it.

"Kenneth, you're our son," his dad said, "and we're very proud of you. We only discipline you and stay after you because we want the best for you."

Ken nodded. "I know, Dad. But when all I hear about is what needs to change, I get discouraged. It's like the other night, when you took away my CD player. I was working on my homework, and it was half done. But you didn't see that. Instead, all I heard about was how bad my music and study habits are."

Doug cut in respectfully. "Ken, maybe it would help if you told your dad what you'd like to hear him say in a situation like the other night's."

Ken thought for a moment. Then, turning toward his dad, he said, "I would have felt better if you said something like, 'How is your homework going?' And when I showed you my worksheet, you might say, 'Good job so far. If you need any help, ask me. Just don't let the music distract you.'"

Feeling more confident, Ken watched his dad process his comment. After several moments, his father began to nod. "I think I see what you mean, Son. I didn't realize I was so one-sided. I'm sorry I was so hard on you the other night, and at other times too. I guess I am so eager for you to succeed that I forget to notice when you *do* succeed. I'm very sorry, Ken. Will you forgive me?"

Before Ken could respond, his mother also apologized for not being more approving and asked his forgiveness. When Ken verbalized his forgiveness, Mom said, "We will do our best to notice your strengths and good behavior and mention them to you."

Greatly encouraged by his parents' positive response, Ken went on to his second big need: for their attention. He explained the loneliness and frustration he felt when they didn't listen to him, spend time with him, or show an interest in his activities. "It would be great sometimes," he concluded, "if you could just come into my room, ask how I'm doing, and listen to me." His parents apologized again and promised to be more attentive.

Ken was prepared to stop there. He could hardly believe his parents' positive response to his words, and he didn't want to overburden them with his feelings. But Mom said, "This is very helpful to us, Kenneth. We didn't know how hurt you were feeling. Is there anything else?"

"Well, maybe one more thing," he said, glancing at Doug for another boost of courage. "When Doug and I talked, I realized I also have a big need for . . . affection. I'm not a kid anymore, and I don't need to hold your hand everywhere we go. But I kind of miss the hugs, and I still like to hear you say 'I love you.'"

Ken's mother was on her feet immediately. She approached him with tears filling her eyes. "I'm so happy to hear you say that, Son. I haven't hugged you as much lately because I thought you didn't want to be treated like a child. I have a lot more hugs and kisses for you."

Standing to meet her, Ken received his mom's tearful embrace. In seconds Dad was there, too, and they all held each other until the three of them were crying. Then Doug Shaw joined in and prayed a short prayer for the Meyers family.

"There's just one thing," Ken said, wiping away tears with the back of his hand. There was a smile of mischief on his face. "I want hugs and kisses, but not when my friends are around, OK?" The four of them enjoyed a good, long laugh.

A few minutes later, when Doug explained that he had to leave, Ken walked him to the front door. "Thanks, Doug, thanks a lot for . . . you know . . . just, thanks."

"No problem, Ken," Doug returned. "I think it turned out well. You did a great job, and your parents . . . well, I think they really love you."

Ken grinned and nodded.

Doug opened the door and stepped out on the porch, then he turned to face his young friend. "Are you feeling OK about talking to Todd? Do you want me to go with you?"

Ken thought for a moment. "Thanks for offering, Doug, but I'll be OK. Talking to my folks today really helped me to see how I need to talk to Todd. I think I can do it by myself . . . except for your prayers, of course."

"I know you can do it, Ken," Doug affirmed as he stepped off the porch, "and I will be praying for you. Just let me know how it turns out." Then he waved and turned toward his car.

"Will do," Ken called after him. Closing the door, he was almost excited about clearing the air with his friend Todd. And he would enjoy talking to Doug—and his parents—about the meeting afterward.

TIME OUT TO CONSIDER

Once you have identified two or three emotional needs that are not being fully met at home, it is time to plan a meeting with your parents to share those needs. This step may sound difficult and frightening, especially if you are not comfortable being so vulnerable with people. But it is necessary if you want your relationship with Dad and Mom to improve.

Here are several steps that will help you prepare for and carry out such a meeting.

Decide if you want someone else to go with you. Ken was grateful to have the counsel and encouragement of his youth leader Doug Shaw. Perhaps you would feel more confident about meeting with your parents if someone joined you. If you have shared your hurt with a youth leader, mature friend, or minister, that person may be willing to go along when you meet with your parents.

Schedule a time to meet. Find a time and place for your meeting that will be free from interruptions and distractions. You might say to your parents, "I have something important I want to talk to you about. What would be a good time and place to sit down and talk for an hour?" Try to set up the meeting as soon as possible, while your unmet emotional needs are fresh in your mind.

Prepare prayerfully. Ask God to give you a pure heart and good attitude for sharing. Ask Him to help you express your thoughts and concerns lovingly and in ways your parents will clearly understand and readily receive. Then decide what you are going to say

27

ahead of time. You may even want to write down your thoughts so you can read them to your parents.

Express your love. Begin the meeting by verbalizing your love and gratitude for your parents. Focus on the positive aspects of your relationship. Thank them for what they do for you. Assure them that you are interested in seeing your relationship grow even stronger and more fulfilling.

Share your unmet emotional needs. Stay away from accusative "you" statements: "You make me so angry"; "You never spend any time with me"; or "You love my brother/sister more than me." Instead, express how you feel with less threatening "I" statements: "I feel ignored and alone when we don't spend time together"; or "I like it when I hear compliments from you."

Ask for—don't demand—their assistance. Say something like, "Dad and Mom, will you help me improve our relationship by trying to meet more of my need for respect?"

Offer to make changes in your behavior. Ask your parents how you can improve the relationship, for example, by being more respectful, affectionate, or accepting. Tell them you are committed to changing your behavior in order to improve the relationship with them.

Pray together. Consider asking your parents to pray with you about your relationship. Ask God for His guidance and help as you seek to be more considerate of each other's needs.

In the weeks following Ken's big meeting with his parents, their relationship began to improve. His parents became more considerate about commenting on Ken's good behavior, spent more time with him, and gave him more hugs. Ken consciously worked at being more appreciative of his parents' love and provision for him. Whenever Dad or Mom displayed approval, attention, or affection, he thanked them for it.

Encouraged by his parents' response, Ken prepared to talk to Todd in much the same way as he had prepared to talk to his parents. He realized that Todd was not meeting his need for respect as a friend, and he prayed that God would help him convey this concern to Todd. When they met, Todd was not as eager to deal with their differences as Ken's parents had been. But Ken felt good about their talk and determined to keep praying that his friendship with Todd would grow stronger.

Ken's relationship with his parents is not perfect. They still experience misunderstandings and disagreements from time to time. But things are getting much better since Ken respectfully sought his parents' help in meeting his needs. And Ken has the same hopes for his friendship with Todd.

There is hope for your relationships too. It all begins with identifying your hurts and needs, sharing them with your parents or friend, and helping each other make the relationship better.

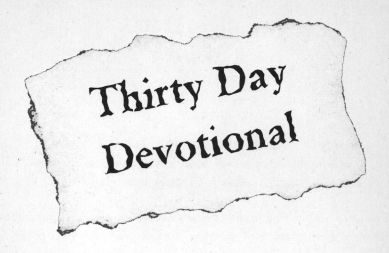

Thirty Day
Devotional

Day 1
Resolve, Don't Dissolve

READ: PHILIPPIANS 2:1–11

Do nothing out of selfish ambition or vain conceit, but in humility consider others better than yourselves (Phil. 2:3).

How can you be true to the person God made you to be and still be at peace with others? Not many students succeed in conflict-proofing their relationships. The very fact that we are different makes conflict inevitable. We bring different backgrounds, viewpoints, emotions, and even different cultures into our relationships. Whenever two people are in some kind of relationship, there will be conflict sooner or later. *Having* conflicts with your parents, siblings, teachers, neighbors, friends, or bosses is not the issue. The real challenge is whether you can *resolve* the conflicts that are inevitable.

As the closeness in relationships grows, so does the potential for conflicts. Working through the maze of misunderstanding and conflict can seem more difficult than getting two warring nations to conduct peace talks. You may begin to wonder if getting close to others is worth it. The closer you get, the more you seem to run into conflicts. And the more conflicts you encounter, the more you wonder if you should look for a way out of the relationship.

There is a phrase I want you to remember: *It is more rewarding to resolve a conflict than to dissolve a relationship.* Of course, it is much easier just to walk away than to put out the effort to resolve a conflict. But the reward of staying is that every time you resolve a conflict you come out a better person—better able to deal with other inevitable conflicts that will come along.

Sometimes we forget that relationships are part of God's design for His human creation. In Genesis 2:18, God says, "It is not good for the man to be alone." This verse was first written for husbands and wives. But I believe that God is also speaking here beyond the marriage relationship. You and I were created not to be alone, but to have relationships. In order to experience the blessing that God intended us to have in our families and friendships, we must go against the temptation to bail out when the heat is on.

We live in a self-centered culture. Society's emphasis is clearly on pleasing ourselves, not on nurturing our relationships. If winning is everything to you, you may reach a few personal goals, but you will sacrifice relationships along the way. Relationships are built by yielding, not winning. So we must rise above our culture and resolve our conflicts—not dissolve our relationships—if we truly want to experience intimate, fulfilling relationships.

My Journal Journey

REFLECT

"When I think about God's design for resolving conflicts instead of dissolving difficult relationships, I feel . . ."

_____

_____

_____

RESPOND

What will it take on your part to make you a better "resolver" of relational conflicts?

_____

_____

_____

PRAY

Talk to God in your own words about a current relational conflict that needs to be resolved.

_____

_____

_____

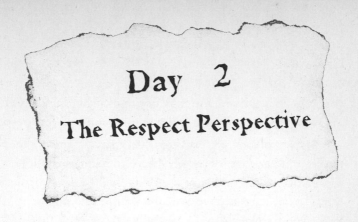

Day 2
The Respect Perspective

READ: PROVERBS 6:16–24

My son, keep your father's commands and do not forsake your mother's teaching (Prov. 6:20).

How would your friends feel if you treated them like you treat your parents? Would you still have many friends? Could your attitude and actions at home be a cause of friction between you and your parents? Good behavior at home isn't enough if the attitude isn't right. God, as well as your parents, want you to have both. Obedience has to do with actions; honor and respect have to do with attitude. You need both.

How can you show your parents that you respect them? The book of Proverbs supplies four different ways.

1. *Respectful speaking.* Proverbs 20:20 says, "If a man curses his father or mother, his lamp will be snuffed out in pitch darkness." There is more to cursing parents than shouting bad words at them. Snipping at them, criticizing them, or simply clamming up when they want you to talk can be disrespectful. And when you talk to them, avoid whining, complaining, and yelling.

2. *Respectful listening.* Proverbs 5:7 says, "Now then, my sons, listen to me; do not turn aside from what I say." When you listen to your parents, really listen. "Turn aside" can mean anything less than eye-to-eye contact and full attention when Dad or Mom have something to say. You may be busy,

you may be in a rush, you may not think what they have to say is important. But your full attention conveys your respect.

3. *Respectful looking.* Proverbs 30:17 says, "The eye that mocks a father, that scorns obedience to a mother, will be pecked out by the ravens of the valley, will be eaten by the vultures." Your parents have probably cautioned you about "the look" you flash at them occasionally. It's the look that says, "That's dumb" or "You're stupid" or "I wish I could trade you in for new parents." Maybe you didn't *say* anything disrespectful, but in God's eyes a disrespectful look is just as bad.

4. *Respectful acting.* Proverbs 6:20 says, "My son, keep your father's commands and do not forsake your mother's teaching." The true test of respectful acting is to follow through on your parents' instructions even when they are not watching. That's a respectful attitude.

Showing your parents that you love them and respect them may not be easy. But it helps keep the conflicts at home to a minimum. And one day when they are gone, you will have some fantastic guilt-free memories.

My Journal Journey

REFLECT

As you read about the topic of respect for parents, what thoughts and feelings stirred inside you?

_____

_____

_____

RESPOND

Respectful speaking, listening, looking, and acting: Which seems to be the most difficult for you? How do you want to change in this area?

_____

_____

_____

PRAY

"Lord, in order to grow into a more respectful person, I need Your help in . . ."

_____

_____

_____

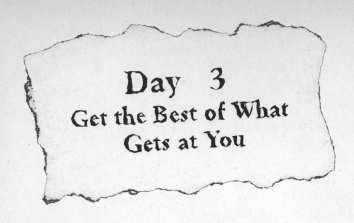

Day 3
Get the Best of What Gets at You

READ: 1 PETER 3:8–17

Do not repay evil with evil or insult with insult, but with blessing, because to this you were called so that you may inherit a blessing (1 Pet. 3:9).

Is there anything you can do when personalities clash between you and family members or friends? Yes, here are some specific actions you can take that will help you get through the conflict.

Get the facts. First, search the Bible about the area of conflict you are experiencing. I have often been able to find situations in the Bible similar to the one I'm going through. Second, get all the information you can about the other person and your conflict with him or her (see Prov. 18:13). Many conflicts arise from misunderstandings and false assumptions about something that was said or done.

Pray. Pray for wisdom about what to do (see James 1:5). Pray for the other person by name. God will change your attitude toward the individual and enable you to deal with the problem better. And pray for that person's success. Peter reminds us not to return evil for evil but to give a blessing to others.

Seek wise counsel. Proverbs 12:15 says, "The way of a fool seems right to him, but a wise man listens to advice." In the story you read earlier, Ken Meyers made a wise choice to talk to Doug Shaw about his problems with his parents. Is there someone like Doug you can talk to, such as a youth leader or a mature Christian friend? Be cautious not to seek counsel only from those who will agree with you or will want to help you "win," but also from those who will help you resolve the conflict.

Deal with your own emotions first. Ephesians 4:26 is a good guideline: "Do not let the sun go down while you are still angry." This verse does not forbid anger, but rather it instructs us to deal with it promptly. If you don't control your anger, it will control you. Those feelings of anger and hurt that have not been resolved will stir your imagination, and as time goes by the facts will become more and more distorted, and bitterness will set in. If you don't deal with your emotions immediately, you will give the devil a foothold in your life (see Eph. 4:27).

Wait for God's timing. Proverbs 15:23 says, "It is wonderful to say the right thing at the right time!" (NLT). I also like verse 28: "The godly think before speaking; the wicked spout evil words" (NLT). My doctor says the reason I don't have an ulcer is because I laugh a lot and because I tell people what I think. I do both, but in speaking my mind I always try to wait for the right time, for a calm emotional state, and for the right motivation.

MY JOURNAL JOURNEY

REFLECT

Which of the Scripture verses above touched you most deeply? What did that verse say to you?

_____

_____

_____

RESPOND

As you think about the tips for helping you to get through conflict, which of them are the most difficult for you? Why?

_____

_____

_____

PRAY

"God, after reading this devotional I am encouraged to . . ."

_____

_____

_____

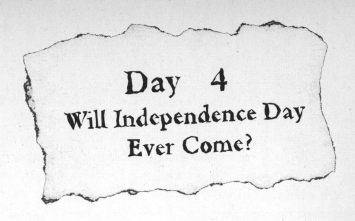

Day 4
Will Independence Day Ever Come?

There is no fear in love. But perfect love drives out fear
(1 John 4:18).

Kelsey is fourteen years old and she just wants some space. She is well on her way to being a young adult, but her mom and dad still treat her like a little kid. She wants to date; her parents say no. She wants to stay up later at night; her parents say no. She wants to sleep over at her friend's house more; her parents say no. Kelsey is really getting angry at them. She fumes, "How can I get them to let go a little and allow me to grow up?"

Does Kelsey's story sound familiar? Are you struggling for your independence at home too? You want to have more freedom. You want to make your own decisions. But your parents are not letting go of the controls as fast as you want them to. And you want to know why. There are a couple of reasons.

First, even though you are becoming an adult, sometimes you still act like a child. When your parents think of turning the keys of control over to you, images of you being an adult don't always flash across their minds. Instead, they remember you as a three-year-old crashing your tricycle into the only tree in the entire yard. What reinforces these pictures are the times when you revert into a whining, obnoxious kid. Your parents must have a new set of images about you before they will turn you loose completely. And this will take some time.

Second, your parents really love you and may not want you to grow up too fast. They enjoy having you around and dependent on them. They realize they only have a few short years left with you at home. To you that may seem like forever. But to them time flies by quickly. They may try to slow the inevitable by not letting go. And that's why they are struggling over letting you be more independent.

What can you do? First, keep talking to God about it. Ask Him for wisdom, patience, and especially love and understanding toward your parents. Next, share your concern with a caring, mature Christian friend or youth leader. Ask that person to help you brainstorm ways you can honor your parents—and perhaps understand them better—while still exploring your possibilities for gradual independence.

Here's another idea. Consider writing a respectful letter to your parents expressing your appreciation for them and listing your concerns, frustrations, and even your proposals for resolving your differences over curfews, dating, and so on. Describe ways you intend to prove your trustworthiness to them. Ask them to help you work toward these goals. Prayerfully plan a time when you can read the letter to your parents and discuss it with them. This could be the beginning of a better relationship with your parents and new opportunities of freedom for you.

My Journal Journey

REFLECT

In what ways does Kelsey's story parallel your relationship with your parents? Describe your own home situation in writing.

_____

_____

_____

RESPOND

"In my own 'struggle' for independence at home, the steps I most need to put into practice are . . ."

_____

_____

_____

PRAY

Write a prayer asking God to guide your parents in the task of preparing you for independence.

_____

_____

_____

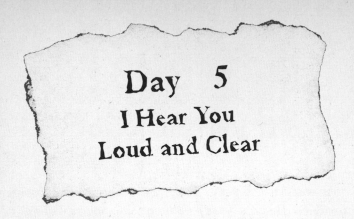

Day 5
I Hear You Loud and Clear

READ: JAMES 1:16–27
Everyone should be quick to listen, slow to speak and slow to become angry (James 1:19).

Most people think of talking as communication—with the goal of getting their point of view across. Meaningful communication, however, has two main parts: talking *and* listening. The part most neglected in relationships today is listening. When one or the other in a relationship lacks the ability to really listen, frustrations set in that will grow into serious relational conflicts if not dealt with.

God gave us two ears but only one mouth, so the Irish have drawn the thoughtful conclusion that we should listen twice as much as we speak. James urges us to be "quick to listen, slow to speak." Shakespeare echoed this principle in his line in *Hamlet*, "Give every man thy ear, but few thy voice." The phrase "quick to listen" means to be a ready listener. Most people are a lot more comfortable in communication when they are doing the talking. Listening is the most difficult aspect of communication for most people. Listening never comes naturally.

Extroverts (like me!) are often especially guilty of talking too much and not listening enough. It's a problem that I'm still working on in my marriage. About eight months after Dottie and I were married, she came to me rather hesitantly. I could tell she was hurting. "I don't think you love me," she confessed.

"What?" I exclaimed. "You've got to be kidding! I love you more than anyone else on the face of the earth."

44

"Honey," she replied, "I really don't think you are interested in some of the things in my life that interest me. I don't think you care about some of the 'little' areas."

Ouch! That was like driving a knife through my heart. Immediately I insisted, "But I do too!"

I was amazed as Dottie explained why she felt that way. "You never listen to me. I will start to share something with you, and you will cut me off or change the subject. Or I will start to share something with you, and your mind wanders off somewhere else. You often pretend that you're listening, but your mind is a thousand miles away."

Since I had not made a serious effort (and sometimes no effort at all) to listen to Dottie, I was communicating to her that what she had to say wasn't important to me. What a way to strangle someone's enthusiasm! Really listening says to another person, "You are important! You are of great value!" Respect for others—your parents, your boyfriend or girlfriend, your teachers, and so on—begins with listening.

My Journal Journey

REFLECT

"When I think about the Bible's command to be 'quick to listen, slow to speak,' I feel . . ."

_____

_____

_____

RESPOND

In what ways do you need to improve as a listener? In which relationships do you most need to improve your listening skills? Write about it.

_____

_____

_____

PRAY

"Thank You, Lord, for listening to me. In order to grow as a listener, I need Your help to . . ."

_____

_____

_____

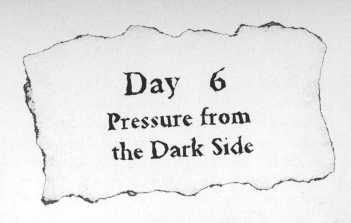

Day 6
Pressure from the Dark Side

READ: HEBREWS 4:12–16

[Jesus] has been tempted in every way, just as we are—yet was without sin (Heb. 4:15).

Randy and his family moved to a new town the summer before he started eighth grade. He might have said no to the cigarette he was offered on the walk home from school—if he had still been in his old school. But he was determined to make friends quickly here, so he took the cigarette and the three new friends who came with it.

When Randy's friends discovered that both his parents worked, leaving him home alone for several hours after school, they began walking home with him or dropping by soon after school let out. Randy knew his parents didn't allow him to have friends in the house when they weren't home, but he always made sure everyone left in time for him to straighten the house before Mom and Dad arrived.

One afternoon, Darren, the guy who had first offered Randy the cigarette, brought a six-pack of beer with him. Randy was already frustrated at the way things were going with his new friends, but he didn't want to tell Darren, so he and his friends smoked and drank beer in the house until Randy pleaded with them to leave. Randy managed to ditch the beer cans before his parents arrived, but the house still smelled of cigarette smoke. His parents accused him of smoking, which he denied. A heated argument followed, and Randy's father grounded him. Randy wished his family had never moved to this town.

Much of your behavior is influenced by peer pressure. Every

47

day you face severe pressure at school and around kids your age to act in certain ways, talk in certain ways, dress in certain ways, join certain groups, and try certain activities. And if you don't go along with what the kids closest to you are doing, you may face ridicule or rejection—and nobody wants to be laughed at or rejected.

Peer pressure can be either negative or positive. Church youth groups, Christian friends, and older brothers and sisters, for example, can be positive influences on you. They can "pressure" you to act compassionately toward people who are hurting. They can "pressure" you to attend Bible study regularly and maintain a daily quiet time. They can even "pressure" you to consider the claims of Christ on your life. But peer pressure can also be negative, and negative peer pressure from your friends and others can be the source of conflict in your relationships.

Did you know that Jesus faced negative peer pressure? Hebrews 4:15 says that He faced the same temptations we face but without sin. He knows what you're going through because He went through it Himself—and He made it! Welcome His presence and power in your life every day. He will help you to withstand the pressures you encounter to do the wrong thing.

My Journal Journey

REFLECT

When you consider that Jesus experienced negative peer pressure, and that He understands the peer pressure you feel, what does it do to you inside?

_____

_____

_____

RESPOND

What are the sources of positive peer pressure in your life at this time? What are the sources of negative peer pressure?

_____

_____

_____

PRAY

"Dear Lord, I need Your presence and power as I face the pressure to . . ."

_____

_____

_____

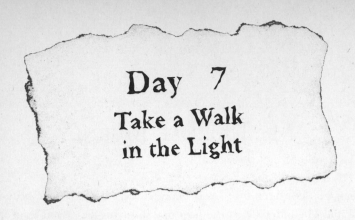

Day 7
Take a Walk in the Light

READ: PHILIPPIANS 4:1–9

Finally, brothers, whatever is true, whatever is noble, whatever is right, whatever is pure, whatever is lovely, whatever is admirable—if anything is excellent or praiseworthy—think about such things (Phil. 4:8).

Like Ken Meyers in the story, you may be struggling with conflicts at home. It may seem that every time you turn around, your parents are chipping at you for something or a brother or sister is testing your patience to the breaking point. Some days it may feel so bad that you wish you could resign from your family.

It is very important to look on the bright side when you are hassled by conflicts. Don't always think about how unreasonable your parents seem to be acting or how much you wish you could trade your little brother in on a new video game. Paul's instruction in Philippians 4:8 is very wise. Keep your attention focused on the positive things in your family relationships. Think about the many good things your parents do for you. Think about the fun times you have with your siblings. Life isn't all hassles and bad news, even though it sometimes seems that way.

Carefully ask yourself these questions. How you answer them says a lot about how you handle conflict at home.

Do I spend more time mentally criticizing my family members than looking at their good points?

Do I bad-mouth my parents or siblings behind their backs?

Do I have a standard for my family members that I can't live up to myself?

Do I pressure family members to conform to my standards so that I can accept them more easily?

There are people in my life who accept me just the way I am. Although they encourage me to become a better person, I know they will not love me any less if I never do. They dwell on the positives, not the negatives. Maybe you need to make more of an effort to focus on the good, especially when conflict situations arise at home.

How can you do this? Make sure the Holy Spirit is in control of your life. If you are not empowered by the Holy Spirit, you will find it difficult, if not impossible, to focus on the positive in your relationships. He is the source who will enable you to apply consistently what you have learned about resolving conflicts. He will also lead you forward to new insights still to be understood.

My Journal Journey

REFLECT

As you asked yourself the four questions above, what do your answers reveal about your attitude at home?

_____

_____

_____

RESPOND

"I want to think and act more positively in my relationships, specifically . . ."

_____

_____

_____

PRAY

Spend some time writing your thanks to God for all the positive qualities you see in your family members.

_____

_____

_____

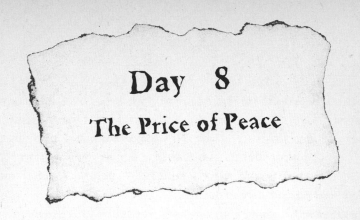

Day 8
The Price of Peace

READ: ROMANS 12:10–21

If it is possible, as far as it depends on you, live at peace with everyone (Rom. 12:18).

I've had so many kids come up to me and ask something like this: "Josh, why do my parents make such a big deal about my appearance, my friends, and my music?" Let's talk about each of them separately.

Your appearance. Parents make a big deal about the way you look for the same reason you make a big deal about the way they look. Think about it. When your friends are over, why do you panic if you think your parents are going to be around? Because you're afraid your friends might think you have weird parents, right? You don't really care if people *like* your parents or not, just as long as your friends *think* they are normal human beings.

The same is true for your parents. They want their friends to think you are a "normal" kid, and they *don't* want their friends to think you're weird. To most parents, a normal kid doesn't dress in studded black leather, dye his hair fluorescent pink, and pierce his body parts with metal objects. So if your clothes and hair are a problem to them, you can help keep the peace at home by not pushing these issues too hard.

Your friends. The main reason parents are concerned about your friends is because they are afraid someone will be a bad influence on you. They know (possibly from experience) how easy it is to pick up bad habits, and they don't want you to get into trouble. They may also be thinking that certain friends aren't good enough

53

for you. Perhaps the underlying reason for their concern is that your parents want the best for you, and very few of your friends can measure up to their standards. This issue, like many others in your relationship with your parents, can be a reason to either start World War III or discuss your feelings peacefully. Choose the latter and be glad your parents care about you.

Your music. Some parents don't want their kids listening to the wild music of the youth culture. One reason has to do with the volume level of your music. Even you have to admit that when your house can be seen shaking from across the street, the music is a little too loud. Put yourself in their shoes. Imagine having to listen to *their* music at maximum volume. You would do a little complaining yourself. They may also be concerned about how you use your time. A lot of students go to an extreme and waste a lot of time listening to music when they could be doing homework, finishing their chores, and so on.

In these issues (and others like them), you have a choice. You can make life difficult at home by pushing hard for your way. Or you can help keep things peaceful by compromising to keep your parents satisfied. It's not peace at any price, but backing off a little on a few issues may make life more enjoyable for everyone.

My Journal Journey

REFLECT

Write out your concerns about your parents' reactions to your appearance, friends, and music.

_____

_____

_____

RESPOND

What are some ways you could better "live at peace with everyone" in your home?

_____

_____

_____

PRAY

"God, transform me into a peacemaker in my home, especially . . ."

_____

_____

_____

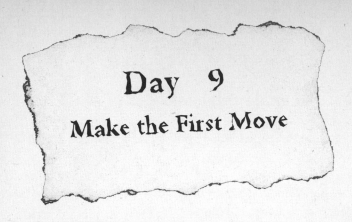

Day 9
Make the First Move

Therefore, if you are offering your gift at the altar and there remember that your brother has something against you, leave your gift there in front of the altar. First go and be reconciled to your brother; then come and offer your gift (Matt. 5:23–24).

When a disagreement is not handled properly, people react in ways that really hurt friendships. Do any of these responses sound familiar?

The silent treatment. People who use this tactic become very quiet when things don't go their way. When asked, "What's wrong?" their standard reply is, "Nothing." Generally they assume the fighting stance of arms crossed, teeth clenched, and eyes staring straight ahead.

Blow 'em away. This style is explosive. When upset, people who use this response start yelling and screaming. If you are unfortunate enough to catch one of them in action, you will easily recognize this behavior. Such people break things, stomp around, wave their arms wildly, and scream bloody murder.

Cry till I die. When conflict arises, some people begin to cry . . . and cry and cry. The other person feels sorry for this poor puddle of tears and gives in out of pity. This approach is successful if a person's goal is to get his or her way.

Smart-mouth. Some people resort to sarcasm when they are on the warpath. Their comments can be biting and stinging and are often accompanied by a recognizable stance: a cocky head position and a turned-up nose.

Go for the throat. When upset, some people go for the kill. They have no mercy. They let you know every fault. They tell you everything you have done wrong. They tear you down, then rip you up.

Turn and run. Instead of fighting, some people run, avoiding conflicts at all costs. To them, fighting is frightening. At the first sign of trouble they head for the hills. If they can't run physically, they withdraw into a shell.[1]

When a friend responds in any of these ways, he or she erects a huge wall that must be dismantled before your friendship can return to normal. Another wall inside you must also be overcome. It's called pride! You think, *No way am I going to try to make things right. He started it. I'm waiting until he comes crawling back to me.*

To get the relationship right, you must first humble yourself and go to your friend. Apologize for any ways you have acted like a jerk. Friendships are too precious for the two of you to stay mad. Make the first move and make it quickly.

My Journal Journey

REFLECT

As you read today's Scripture passage, what caught your attention and challenged you about your relationships?

RESPOND

"When someone responds to me in one of the negative ways described above, I will . . ."

PRAY

"Lord, keep me from responding to conflicts in a negative way, especially . . ."

Day 10
Giving Your Love Away

READ: JOHN 15:9–17

Greater love has no one than this, that he lay down his life for his friends (John 15:13).

The commonly held attitude, "I want what I want when I want it," is the at the heart of most conflicts between people. This self-centered force destroys friendships, marriages, and families. I believe we could solve a majority of people problems today if we could only develop an attitude of giving instead of taking, of putting others' needs first.

A maximum relationship with your parents, siblings, friends, and others involves giving 100 percent, no matter what the response is. Most of us want a fifty/fifty arrangement in our relationships: "I'll give my part if you give your part." The problem with a fifty/fifty deal is that you are always trying to decide whether the other person has done his or her part. Somehow it never seems to be enough. When you give 100 percent, you are free to accept that other person unconditionally.

There is a wonderful reward when you make giving a priority in your relationships. You will find that when you give 100 percent, you get back 150 percent. When someone feels unconditionally loved, he or she can't help but respond with the same kind of love. You will always get back more than you give.

When your love for others is true, you will not only be concerned about getting your needs met. You will also be equally concerned about fulfilling the needs of others. And when those needs seem to clash with yours, true love does not have to flip a coin to decide whose needs will be taken care of first. True love, the love that gives, desires to reach out to the other person first. You will find that the needs of others are more important than your own.

When your focus is on giving to others, you will take their feelings and opinions into consideration when you make decisions. Love that gives is willing to sacrifice. When you really care about someone's happiness and growth, you will be willing to back up your love with actions.

Our model for giving love is Jesus Christ. His love made Him willing to sacrifice. He was a living example of His teaching on love. The purpose of Jesus' life and death on the cross was not only our salvation, but also to fill our lives with joy (John 15:11). Following Christ's example, Paul wrote, "Each of us should please his neighbor for his good, to build him up" (Rom. 15:2). Your love for the people in your life is mature when you care more about the relationship and the other person than about your own desires. Conflicts in your relationships will diminish when common goals become a priority and when winning and proving yourself right is not important to you.

My Journal Journey

REFLECT

What happens inside you when you consider that Jesus' purpose for coming to earth was to give you forgiveness and joy?

_____

_____

_____

RESPOND

"In order to follow Christ's example of giving love in my relation-ships, I need to . . ."

_____

_____

_____

PRAY

Tell God in your own words how you feel about His Son laying down His life for you.

_____

_____

_____

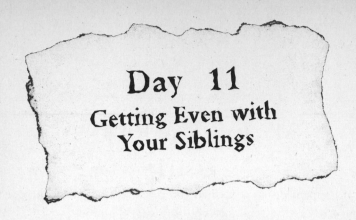

Day 11
Getting Even with Your Siblings

READ: LUKE 6:27–36

Love your enemies, do good to those who hate you, bless those who curse you, pray for those who mistreat you (Luke 6:27–28).

For years, Sabrina and her older brother, Mike, were best friends. They played football and baseball together. They went bicycling with each other. They were much closer to each other than either was to their older sister. But that all changed around the time Sabrina turned fourteen. Her interests began to change. It wasn't as much fun to hang out with Mike anymore; instead, she found herself drawn to her sister. She suddenly seemed to have much more in common with her than with Mike.

That's when Mike started with the insults. "He would call me 'snout,' then 'flea-festation,'" said Sabrina. "I hated it, and I didn't know why he was behaving the way he was. All of a sudden, he wasn't my best friend. If he knew something bothered me, he'd keep going on and on about it until I'd get even more upset and start to cry. It really hurt, and I didn't know why it was happening. It was awful."

Sabrina's experience is pretty common. Brothers and sisters can be best friends, bitter enemies—or both, depending on the circumstances, the time of day, or their moods. Siblings can be loving toward each other one day and cruel the next. Does this sound familiar? Have you experienced irritations and conflicts with a brother or sister? Are you involved in a sibling rivalry?

It can irritate even the most mature young people to come home and find that a brother or sister has been in their room uninvited or has messed with their clothes or CDs. So what should you do in such a situation? As the saying goes, "Don't get mad, get even!" Now that doesn't mean to behave in kind to your sibling. Luke 6:27–31 offers a few simple suggestions on how God wants you to "get even" with your brother or sister. If he or she hates you, insults you, hits you, wears some of your clothes without asking, or whatever, your sibling is acting like your enemy. These verses in Luke tell you how to respond.

First, love. That means forgiving instead of paying back.

Second, do good. Return a kind word or deed for an unkind one.

Third, bless. Thank God for your brother or sister in spite of the conflict.

Fourth, pray. Ask God to help you resolve the conflict.

Fifth, turn the other cheek. Striking back will only escalate the problem.

This approach may not be as easy as lashing out and giving back what your brother or sister has done to you. But as you practice this biblical response, you will discover that life at home will be a lot happier.

My Journal Journey

REFLECT

"The biblical pattern for handling conflicts with 'enemies' hits me as . . ."

_____

_____

_____

RESPOND

"In order to create a happier environment between me and my sibling(s), I need to . . ."

_____

_____

_____

PRAY

Spend some time writing a prayer to God on the subject of your sibling(s). Tell God how you feel about any conflicts you are experiencing. Talk to Him about how you want your relationships at home to improve.

_____

_____

_____

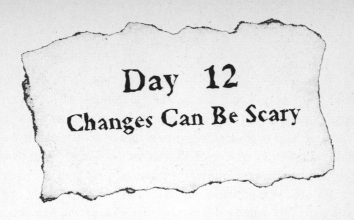

Day 12
Changes Can Be Scary

READ: ISAIAH 40:21–31

Even youths grow tired and weary, and young men stumble and fall; but those who hope in the LORD will renew their strength. They will soar on wings like eagles; they will run and not grow weary, they will walk and not be faint (Isa. 40:30–31).

"Why do my parents sometimes look at me like I'm some kind of alien from another planet?" Maybe you have asked yourself something similar. Well, in a word, your parents may be bug-eyed at you sometimes because you have changed. Consider your appetite, for example. When you were a little kid, they had to coax you to eat your meals. Now you have the appetite of a giant termite, consuming a week's worth of groceries in a matter of hours—usually without the help of your friends. And when your parents dressed you, your little outfits were predictable and "cute." But since you began picking out your own clothes, you have probably come up with some blinding combinations they never expected.

If those two developments are not enough to amaze them, what about your growth rate? They may be somewhat fearful that if you keep growing at this rate, you will be too big for your room. Your intelligence has also increased. You may already be way ahead of your parents in computer skills. If you don't know everything about everything by now, it seems that you soon will—at least that's what they fear.

Once you were polite and well mannered, but now you belch in public and respond to most of their questions with, "Leave me alone." You no longer require any sleep. You go to bed a 4 A.M. and get up at 7. If you are a guy, you never leave your room. If you are a girl, you never come out of the bathroom. These things can be a little threatening. In a matter of months, your parents have witnessed a radical transformation take place in their "little boy" or "little girl." No wonder they sometimes look at you like you are a bit weird.

But don't worry: The same thing happened to them. It's a great time of life that everyone goes through. Parents speak of their own transition years with great memories. Even though they may struggle at times with the big changes taking place in your life right now, they will survive, especially if you give them some time to adjust to the new you. Take Isaiah's advice and put your hope in the Lord. That's the way to renew your strength for getting through the difficulties in your relationship with your parents and others. Make the Lord your source of hope, and He will help you rise above the tough times and misunderstandings. He will get you through this time with your parents, and He will also get them through it.

My Journal Journey

REFLECT

Thinking about your relationships at home and elsewhere, how does Isaiah 40:30–31 encourage you?

_____

_____

_____

RESPOND

How will you nurture your hope in the Lord and apply it to your relationship with your parents?

_____

_____

_____

PRAY

"Guide me and my parents, Lord, as I go through many changes. We especially need Your guidance in . . ."

_____

_____

_____

Day 13
Forgive and Forget

READ: MATTHEW 6:5–15

If you forgive men when they sin against you, your heavenly Father will also forgive you. But if you do not forgive men their sins, your Father will not forgive your sins (Matt. 6:14–15).

Once when I was in Hawaii, a very sharp-looking man and his wife sat down near me. We struck up a conversation, and I asked about his work. He explained that he was a consultant to corporations in the areas of personnel development and problems. When I asked what problem he encountered most, he immediately replied, "Conflict."

So I asked, "What is the number-one way you have found to resolve conflict?"

The man answered immediately, "Forgiveness." He went on to explain that the greatest difficulty he faced was in challenging people to release their bitterness and to give and accept forgiveness in relationship conflicts. This man, who wasn't a Christian, clearly understood the reconciling power of forgiveness.

We are living in a culture overrun with stored-up grudges, resentment, bitterness, and broken hearts. When these hurts are not confronted and resolved, they tear apart relationships, dull the cutting edge of the Holy Spirit in the lives of individuals, and divide families, friendships, marriages, and churches.

Forgiveness is the oil of relationships. It reduces the friction and allows people to come close to one another. If you do not believe another individual is a forgiving person, you can never be truly open and vulnerable to him or her. An unforgiving person cannot develop lasting and intimate relationships. No matter how intelligent or skilled you may be, if you cannot forgive, you cannot develop close relationships. They will be torn apart by unforgotten conflicts because the people involved remain unforgiven.

The Bible is not vague on this issue. We are *commanded* to forgive. In Matthew 6:15 I believe Jesus is saying that if we refuse to forgive people who have wronged us, God will know that our confession of sin is bogus, that we have not really received His forgiveness. Instead, we must forgive others even if they have not changed, just as God paid the price for us while we were still sinners (see Rom. 5:8). And just as God's loving kindness led us to repentance, isn't it possible that our loving kindness to others, expressed through forgiveness, might help lead them to repentance?

Our standard for forgiveness is Christ's forgiveness—absolute and immediate. While still hanging on the cross, He even forgave the people who crucified Him! In situations where we are tempted to lash out at someone who has hurt us, we must remember the constant description of the life of Christ, who forgave all.

My Journal Journey

REFLECT

"When I think about how God has forgiven me for my sins, it makes me feel . . ."

_____

_____

_____

RESPOND

You may be struggling with unforgiveness toward someone in your life. Or you may know of someone who has been unable to forgive you. How will you respond in light of today's devotional?

_____

_____

_____

PRAY

Express to God in writing your gratitude for His forgiveness and your requests for applying forgiveness to your life.

_____

_____

_____

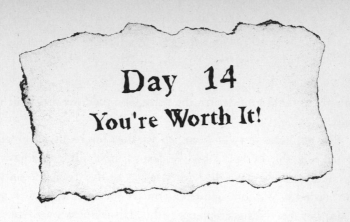

Day 14
You're Worth It!

Look at the birds of the air; they do not sow or reap or store away in barns, and yet your heavenly Father feeds them. Are you not much more valuable than they?
(Matt. 6:26)

Have you ever said, "I really don't count. I could disappear and no one would notice or care"? Most people, including kids your age, think those thoughts at one time or another. It can be the source of tremendous inner conflict. But the Bible reveals that God looks at us quite differently. He sees you as very special because He created you in His image.

Right at the beginning of the Old Testament, God said, "Let us make man in our image, in our likeness" (Gen. 1:26). So He did it. This accounts for our ability to love, to exercise our will, to choose and make moral decisions. Most of us have not really stopped to think about how special that is. Suppose you went outside and stood next to a tree. You could say that in many ways you are equal in value to the tree, since both you and the tree were specially created by God. But there is one critical difference: God created you in His image. God did not give His image to any other part of His creation.

You are also special because you are of great value and worth to God. In 1 Corinthians 6:20, Paul says that we have been purchased with a great price. The value or worth of an object is usually determined by the price someone is willing to pay for it. It couldn't be more true for you or me. If anyone asks what I am worth, I can

71

factually say that I am worth the price God paid for me, which was Jesus.

Before I became a Christian, this realization really humbled me. If I had been the only person alive, Jesus Christ still would have died for me. He would have died for you if you had been the only one who needed it. Without question, you are special and of great value. In Matthew 6:26 Jesus emphasizes this. His followers were having a problem. They were all concerned with what they should wear, what they were going to eat and drink, and where they were going to sleep. And Jesus selected the birds to illustrate His point. He explained that if God cares for the sparrows, He will also care for us because we are worth much more than little birds.

God has made you with great value. You will experience wonderful inner peace as you understand and accept the value God has placed on you. Just be careful to recognize that it is not because of anything you have accomplished. Your value and worth is based upon who Jesus is and what He has done for you. Christ's loving actions on your behalf have demonstrated and documented forever the great value you have to God.

My Journal Journey

REFLECT

Write your thoughts and feelings about the value and worth God has placed on you.

_____

_____

_____

RESPOND

"If God views me as a person of great value and worth, then I must . . ."

_____

_____

_____

PRAY

"Lord, I am humbled to realize that You value me so highly. Help me to apply this realization when . . ."

_____

_____

_____

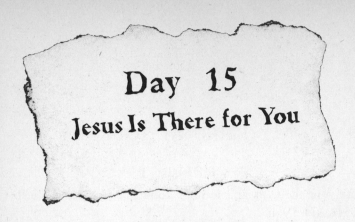

Day 15
Jesus Is There for You

READ: MARK 10:13–16

Let the little children come to me, and do not hinder them,
for the kingdom of God belongs to such as these
(Mark 10:14).

Mark and Debbie were both Christians. They met in the church youth group. Both were sixteen years old when they began dating. They were both sophomores in high school, both had been raised in the same town, and both were good students. They had much in common—but not everything.

Mark was the star basketball player of his high school team and was named to the all-district team. When he won the award as the most valuable player in the district championship tournament, he smiled and swaggered to center court to accept the trophy. Everything about him proclaimed that he thought he deserved the honor—and more. He didn't search the faces in the crowd to find his parents because he knew they wouldn't be there. They never were.

Debbie couldn't understand it. She played on the field hockey team, and her parents never missed a game. In fact, they seldom missed a practice. They seemed to take an intense interest in everything she did.

It wasn't just Mark's sports that his parents missed. His dad was a businessman who traveled a lot, and his mom was an obstetrician. They were highly respected in the community. But most mornings, Mark left for school without seeing his parents, and he usually scrounged in the kitchen to make his own dinner at night. Mark sometimes commented to his youth pastor that he could probably die and his parents wouldn't discover his body until it began to stink up the house.

We are talking here about attentive and inattentive parents. Debbie's parents are very attentive and deeply involved in her life and activities. Mark's parents are largely inattentive and uninvolved in his life and activities. Most kids I know wish their parents were more interested and involved in their lives. Maybe your parents' inattention is a source of conflict between you.

When you feel like your parents are not giving you the attention you want, you need to know that there is someone who is always interested in you. When a crowd of children flocked around Jesus, the disciples wanted to send them away. I guess they thought that Jesus was too busy to give them His time and attention, like some adults are today. But Jesus is always there for kids—then and now. He is always at your game, always there when you get home, always ready to listen when you have a problem. Cherish those times when your parents are available to you and involved in what you're doing. But when they can't be there, remember that Jesus always is.

My Journal Journey

REFLECT

"When I think about Christ's promise to always be here for me, I feel . . ."

_____

_____

_____

RESPOND

In what ways would you like your parents to be more interested and/or involved in your life? How will you communicate your wishes?

_____

_____

_____

PRAY

Write your praise to God for all the ways He demonstrates His involvement in your life.

_____

_____

_____

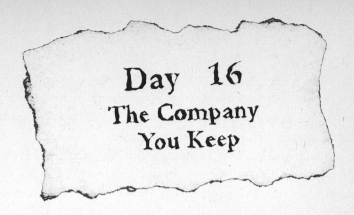

Day 16
The Company You Keep

READ: 2 TIMOTHY 3:1–9

Do not be misled: "Bad company corrupts good character"
(1 Cor. 15:33).

"My parents are always ragging on me about my friends," Darcy said. She was talking to Karen, the adult leader in her youth group. "They say my friends aren't the kind of people they want me hanging out with. What do they want me to do, be friends with Snow White?"

"Your parents probably sense something in your friends' lives that is headed for trouble," Karen replied. "And even though it may bug kids to admit it, parents are usually right about such things. They love you very much, Darcy, and they are sensitive to anything that may be a negative influence on you. And since close friends have so much influence in our lives, you need to be careful who you choose as your closest friends. Choosing your friends wisely will go a long way toward making your parents happy and making you the person God wants you to be."

That's good advice. Right now you are probably a kind, obedient, thoughtful, responsible, maybe even angelic person. But suppose you start hanging out with someone who influences you to become a smart-mouth at home or apathetic at school. When things like that happen, watch out. "Friends" like this are not good for you regardless of how much fun you have together. They have a negative influence on you, and you do not need to be so close to them.

Now this doesn't mean you can't be friends with a rowdy kid or with someone who tends to get into trouble often. As long as you are a positive influence on such people, you can be friends with the rowdiest kid at school. But when someone influences you negatively, 1 Corinthians 15:33 advises you to back off.

How do you back off from an unhealthy friendship? It's never easy, especially if the friend has already been a negative influence on you. You will want to explain why. You might want to say something like this, "You know, Chrissy, I have renewed my commitment to Jesus Christ, and I don't want to disappoint Him anymore by doing the things I have been doing lately. If you want to do those things without me, that's up to you, but I don't want to join you anymore. If you would like to get close to the Lord with me, that would be great! What do you think?"

Remember, it will be tough to back off because of the potential pain of losing a friend. But continuing the friendship would be tougher, especially in the long run, because of your friend's negative influence. Be sure to identify yourself and your decision with Christ. Be humble and gentle in your conversation, yet firm in your decision. Invite your friend to join you in getting closer to Christ. If he or she does not, your friend is the one leaving, not you.

My Journal Journey

REFLECT

How much do you think you are being influenced in the wrong way by some of your friends? What impact is it having on your behavior at home?

_____

_____

_____

RESPOND

Do you have a friend like Chrissy that you need to confront about his or her negative influence in your life? If so, what will you say?

_____

_____

_____

PRAY

Spend some time praying for your friends and how you can be a positive influence in their lives.

_____

_____

_____

Day 17
Taking Trust to the Bank

READ: LUKE 16:1–13

*If you have not been trustworthy in handling worldly wealth,
who will trust you with true riches? And if you have not
been trustworthy with someone else's property, who will give
you property of your own? (Luke 16:11–12).*

Kids often complain to me that their parents don't trust them in
being out late, using the car, being with their friends without adult
supervision, spending their own money wisely, going on dates, making important decisions, buying their own clothes, telling the truth,
completing their chores, or doing their homework. This lack of trust
really angers some kids, putting heat on relationships at home.
Maybe you have felt that way too.

Trust must be earned, especially if you have been untrustworthy
in the past. For your parents to trust you, you must demonstrate
responsible behavior. That means doing what you say you will do
when you say you will do it. Every time you demonstrate that you
are responsible, your parents' trust level rises. The problem is that
trust is like a savings account. Each time you act responsibly, you
make a deposit. Each time you blow a responsibility, you make a
withdrawal. Withdrawals are easy. Deposits represent a lot of hard
work. It seems to take forever to build trust up to a significant level.
But you can drain it down to zero by just doing one stupid thing.

If you want your parents' trust in you to grow, reduce your
withdrawals. Talk to your parents about what ways, if any, you are
losing their trust, then change. Second, follow through on your pres-

ent responsibilities. Be especially concerned with even the seemingly small responsibilities. Your parents probably think like this: "If I can't trust her to do something little like take out the trash, how can I trust her with something bigger like using the car?"

Lying to your parents can drain your trust account faster than anything. To gain your parents' trust, ask them to forgive you for any and every time you have lied to them in the past. And don't stop with just asking forgiveness for the lies you have spoken with your mouth. Also ask forgiveness for the lies you have told with your actions, like having a bunch of friends over at the house when you were told not to.

Also, learn to admit when you blow it. Your parents know that you are not perfect. When they hear you say you goofed up and you are sorry for what you did, they will believe you much more quickly than if you never admit your faults and failures.

My Journal Journey

REFLECT

Are you a trustworthy person at home? In what ways do you think you are? In what ways have you failed to gain your parents' trust?

_____

_____

_____

RESPOND

"In order to begin making 'deposits' in my 'trust account' with my parents, I will . . ."

_____

_____

_____

PRAY

"Lord, work in my life to make me a more trustworthy person, especially . . ."

_____

_____

_____

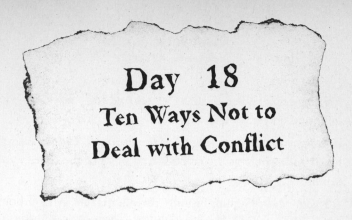

Day 18
Ten Ways Not to Deal with Conflict

READ: ROMANS 5:1–8

As iron sharpens iron, so one man sharpens another
(Prov. 27:17).

Do you know that good feeling you get after a problem between you and someone else has been cleared up? If so, you will agree that positive benefits can come out of conflict. I know that I have become a sharper, more useful instrument in the hands of the Holy Spirit because of how God has used conflicts with people in my life. Romans 5:3–4 explains that tribulation brings about perseverance and proven character. God uses conflicts in my life to develop these inner qualities.

But we sometimes miss these benefits because we respond to conflicts the wrong way. Here are ten unhealthy ways to treat a conflict.

1. *Problem? What problem?* The person or subject of the conflict is ignored and the conflict simply goes unresolved.

2. *The silent treatment.* You don't talk about your conflict and hide out by staying away from the person or source of the conflict.

3. *It's no big deal.* Ignoring the significance of the conflict doesn't make it go away. Instead it can grow into a much larger problem.

4. *Well, all things work together for good.* Over-spiritualizing the problem sometimes means that we're not sincere about resolving it.

5. *Keeping score.* When conflicts, anger, and resentment are bottled up inside, sooner or later somebody will explode.

6. *Attacking the person instead of the problem.* People are to be loved and problems are to be solved; it's not the other way around.

7. *It's your fault.* Blaming usually reveals that the person pointing the finger is unable to admit his or her own failures.

8. *I'm right, you're wrong.* The desire to win at all costs will not resolve anything. Somebody will go away full of resentment.

9. *I surrender.* Giving in just to avoid conflict only keeps the pain alive. No one goes away feeling that something was accomplished.

10. *Bribery.* Instead of dealing with a conflict, some people try to buy their way out of it by offering a special gift.

You will be glad to know that there are also positive and constructive ways of handling interpersonal problems. Each starts with your commitment to the lordship of Jesus Christ. Your desire to resolve conflict will also depend on your commitment to the other person. The closer you are, the more willing you will be to work through the conflict.

My Journal Journey

REFLECT

Think about your commitment to the lordship of Jesus Christ and to the person(s) you may be in conflict with. Then put your thoughts in writing.

_____

_____

_____

RESPOND

"In order to resolve conflicts with others, I need to change the way I respond, specifically . . ."

_____

_____

_____

PRAY

"Lord, I ask Your forgiveness for . . ."

_____

_____

_____

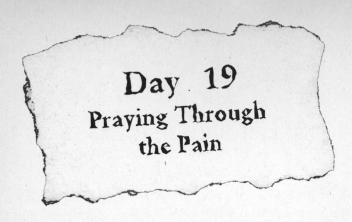

Day 19
Praying Through the Pain

READ: EPHESIANS 6:11–18

For our struggle is not against flesh and blood, but against the rulers, against the authorities, against the powers of this dark world and against the spiritual forces of evil in the heavenly realms (Eph. 6:12).

Sometimes people just don't get along, and this is even true of your parents. There may be a lot of different causes. You may wonder if you are the cause of their disagreements. But the major stress points in a marriage are not kids as much as financial problems or a lack of communication or trust between husband and wife. When two people in a relationship are under pressure, their sensitivity level goes up. As a result, each can be easily hurt by the other. Unresolved pain and distrust can cool their love, and they begin to fight or avoid each other.

One of the deadliest weapons in a couple's arsenal during a disagreement is the topic of divorce. They know that by merely bringing up the subject they can inflict great pain on one another. Perhaps divorce has been threatened in your home or the home of a close friend. Perhaps you already live in a home scarred by divorce. You must realize that you are neither responsible for, nor capable of, keeping a married couple together, not even your parents. You do not cause divorce; neither can you prevent it—and God doesn't expect you to.

God makes it clear in His Word that the victims of broken families are of special concern to Him. Psalm 68:5 says, "A father to the fatherless, a defender of widows, is God in his holy dwelling." And

Psalm 10:14 declares, "But you, O God, do see trouble and grief; you consider it to take it in hand. The victim commits himself to you; you are the helper of the fatherless." God does not frown on those whose parents have left them; He does not turn a deaf ear to the painful cries of those whose families have been shattered by divorce.

What can you do when your parents fight or threaten each other with divorce? First, God commands you to honor and obey your parents just as always (see Exod. 20:12; Eph. 6:1). Family distress and breakup may make it harder to obey God's commands, but these problems do not cancel out His commands.

Second, whenever difficulties arise between your parents (or any other couples you know), go into your room and assume the role of a prayer warrior. Fight in the only way you can: in prayer against the evil forces that threaten to pull two people apart. And don't just settle for one quick prayer and then forget about it. Ephesians 6:18 reminds us to "keep on praying." Turning the battle over to God in prayer doesn't guarantee that your parents will stay together (or get back together if they are divorced). But your prayer will unleash God's best for all concerned in this conflict.

MY JOURNAL JOURNEY

REFLECT

How does it make you feel knowing that God is so compassionate
toward people from broken families?

_____

_____

_____

RESPOND

"I can be more compassionate and helpful toward couples in crisis
by . . ."

_____

_____

_____

PRAY

Spend time now praying for any married couples you know whose
marriages are threatened by divorce.

_____

_____

_____

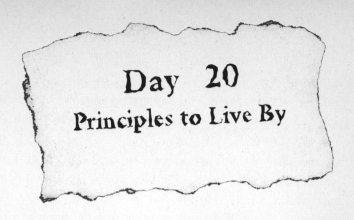

Day 20
Principles to Live By

READ: ROMANS 14:8–13

*Therefore let us stop passing judgment on one another.
Instead, make up your mind not to put any stumbling block
or obstacle in your brother's way (Rom. 14:13).*

I want to share with you some principles I try to live by each day. I don't always succeed, but it is my heart's desire to apply these truths to my life daily, especially in the area of conflicts between people. Perhaps they will help you.

1. *Admit you are not perfect.* Accepting criticism and admitting to your mistakes is one of the first attitudes that will help you to solve your conflicts with people (see Prov. 13:18). So when you are wrong, admit it. When you are right, don't say anything. Paul says in Philippians 1:6, "For I am confident of this very thing, that he who began a good work in you will perfect it until the day of Christ Jesus"(NASB). No mistake you can make will ruin you for life. God is greater than your greatest goofs. And through constructive criticism, He can use our mistakes to make us better individuals and better lovers of Him and other people (see Prov. 28:13). When I have a problem with someone, I pray, "Lord, I want You to resolve this conflict, and please start with me."

2. *Take responsibility for how you feel and how you react.* We can't blame other people for our temper or outbursts of anger. Anger should be our reaction to an unjust situation, not to the

faults of another person. If you keep getting angry with someone else, it may be because you see in that person a fault you also see in yourself.

3. *See the other person's point.* You have probably heard the Native American proverb, "Do not criticize a man until you have walked a mile in his moccasins." It's sound advice. Try to experience the conflict from the other person's point of view. Try to feel what he or she is feeling, not just to see the problem through his or her eyes. You will find that the other person has a good basis for his or her feelings. You have to look beyond your hurt to see the other person's hurt.

Saint Francis of Assisi prayed, "Lord, grant that I may seek more to understand than to be understood." Can you imagine what would happen in our relationships if we all held this attitude? Most conflicts would quickly dissolve because most of them are the result of each of us holding on to our own way of seeing them.

If you want to handle your conflicts in a biblical way, you must remember this question: What does God want to teach me in this conflict? Whatever it is, you can learn from it.

My Journal Journey

REFLECT

Are you in a conflict with someone right now? If so, what do you think God wants to teach you in this conflict?

_____

_____

_____

RESPOND

"The principles in today's section that I most need to apply to the conflicts in my life are . . ."

_____

_____

_____

PRAY

"Lord, help me to understand others and their viewpoints, specifically . . ."

_____

_____

_____

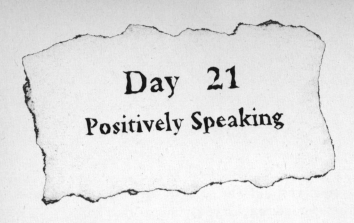

Day 21
Positively Speaking

READ: PROVERBS 23:15–23

Do not let any unwholesome talk come out of your mouths, but only what is helpful for building others up according to their needs, that it may benefit those who listen (Eph. 4:29).

Being positive is a real plus factor in keeping conflicts from ruining your relationships. Being positive helps to keep your relationships open and healthy, while criticism opens the door to conflicts with parents, friends, teachers, and others. Two very critical people can communicate, but it probably will not be healthy communication.

During a three-day lecture series at the University of Tennessee, I was in a meeting with the Campus Crusade staff and several key students. One of the students walked in and said, "I'm not going to hand out any more fliers. Everybody's negative about the meetings. All I've heard is negative responses this morning."

I immediately asked, "How many people have given you a hard time? Twenty-five?"

"No."

"Ten?"

"No."

"Was it five?" I asked.

Again she said, "No."

We discovered that only two people had reacted negatively to the two or three hundred fliers she had handed out. Everyone in the room, including her, realized that she had blown the negative way out of proportion.

In our relationships with others, we tend to remember only the negative from conversations and statements about ourselves. Ten positive statements and one negative statement may be made, but we will remember the negative one the most. The ratio of praise to criticism in a conversation ought to be a healthy 90 percent praise and only 10 percent criticism. Are you a positive communicator in your relationships? It will be far easier for people to reach out to you and share if your attitude, expression, and words are positive.

The apostle Paul gave excellent guidance about the proper emphasis of our attitude and lifestyle when he wrote, "Whatever is true, whatever is noble, whatever is right, whatever is pure, whatever is lovely, whatever is admirable—if anything is excellent or praiseworthy—think about such things" (Phil. 4:8). Be encouraging and let your conversation be positive. It will help to keep your conflicts small and manageable.

MY JOURNAL JOURNEY

REFLECT

"The biblical encouragement to be positive in relationships makes me think about . . ."

_____

_____

_____

RESPOND

Which relationships in your life most need your positive attitude and conversation right now? Write about them and what you will do.

_____

_____

_____

PRAY

"God, I need Your help to become more positive in my relationships, especially . . ."

_____

_____

_____

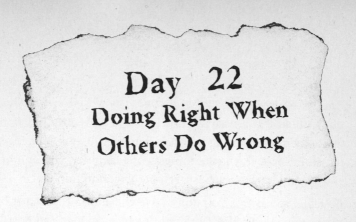

Day 22
Doing Right When Others Do Wrong

READ: PSALM 103:1–14

The LORD is compassionate and gracious, slow to anger, abounding in love (Ps. 103:8).

Peer pressure can be the source of a lot of conflicts in your life. Peer pressure is that powerful influence your friends have that dictates the clothes you wear, the words you use, the people you associate with, the places you go, and the attitudes you have. Positive peer pressure can be good and healthy. But negative peer pressure urges you to say and do things you know you shouldn't say or do.

Peer pressure is powerful because every single person on earth has a God-given need to be loved and accepted. God wants you to find this drive fulfilled in your love relationship with Him and His people. He wants you to be secure in how much He loves and accepts you as His chosen child. If you don't feel His love, you will look to your friends for acceptance. The greater your insecurity, the greater your need for acceptance and the more significant your friends' opinions become.

How can you respond positively to peer pressure, especially negative peer pressure? Here are some suggestions:

1. *Stay close to Jesus Christ and His Word.* That's how you grow in the knowledge of how much He loves you and how totally He accepts you. Spend time in the Bible and in prayer every day. Memorize passages of Scripture, like Psalm 103, that declare God's eternal love for you.

95

2. *Always ask yourself, "What will happen if I give in?"* Always think about the consequences of your actions ahead of time. Is the outcome something that will benefit you and your relationships, or will it make things worse between you and others? If you don't see a positive outcome, don't do it.

3. *Be ready to say no.* You don't have to be a snob about it by saying something like, "I'm not going to do that and be a big heathen like you guys." You can say no without condemning others with words like, "No, thanks, that's not for me."

4. *Stay away from negative pressure situations.* If you find it hard to resist the negative peer pressure at wild parties, don't go to wild parties. If you have a hard time saying no when your friends want to see a movie you shouldn't see, don't go to movies with those friends. You get the idea.

5. *Put yourself in positive pressure situations.* Hang out with the kind of people who make the choices you want to make. This doesn't mean you should avoid non-Christians or people who get into trouble. But allow yourself to be influenced by the right crowd so you can be a positive influence when you're in the wrong crowd.

My Journal Journey

REFLECT

Think and write about the people who influence you most. Who exerts positive peer pressure on you and how? Who exerts negative peer pressure on you and how?

_____

_____

_____

RESPOND

In what ways do you want to be a more positive influence on your friends?

_____

_____

_____

PRAY

Share with God in writing your concerns and needs regarding peer pressure.

_____

_____

_____

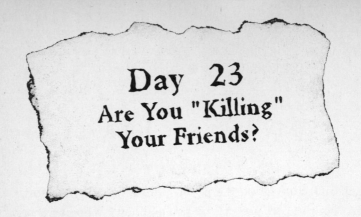

Day 23
Are You "Killing" Your Friends?

READ: 1 THESSALONIANS 5:11–18

Therefore encourage one another and build each other up, just as in fact you are doing (1 Thess. 5:11).

"Whenever I get a close friend, it seems like I always do something to mess it up," Rick lamented. "What am I doing wrong? How can I keep from causing these conflicts?"

Rick—and anybody else who experiences conflicts with friends—needs to know about the things that cause problems in friendships. Once you know about them, you can concentrate on avoiding them. Here are several "friendship killers."

- *Jealousy.* Why not celebrate a friend's achievements and good fortunes instead of envying them?

- *Gossip.* You only bring yourself and your friendships down when you tear others down.

- *Disloyalty.* When you say you are a true friend and then fail to stand by someone under certain circumstances, you may lose your friend.

- *Competition.* Friendship is not about seeing who is best at everything you do. A true friend is there to cheer the other on.

- *Negativism.* Misery loves company—but only up to a point. Beyond that, your complaining will drive your friends away.

- *Selfishness.* Friendship is built on the idea that you have time for others, not just for yourself. If you turn everything toward yourself, you will turn others away.

It takes skill to develop and keep friends. Apply these skills to help you to form friendships that will last.

- *Feel good about yourself.* If you don't like yourself, it will be difficult for anyone else to like you.

- *Accept people for who they are.* Avoid judging or condemning others even if they are sometimes offensive. Overlook their faults. If you accept people for who they are, they are more likely to change for the better.

- *Be positive and encouraging.* Most people live with a lot of criticism. Learn to build people up and you will be a breath of fresh air in their lives.

- *Practice confidentiality.* Stop immediately if you hear yourself saying, "My friend told me not to tell anyone, but I know she won't mind if I tell you."

- *Be a good listener.* Really listen to your friends instead of just waiting for them to shut up so you can say what you want to say.

- *Be patient.* It takes a lot of time to build close and committed friendships.

My Journal Journey

REFLECT

"When I scan the list of '"friendship killers,'" I feel convicted about . . ."

_____

_____

_____

RESPOND

"When I scan the list of skills for developing and keeping friends, I recognize that I especially need to work on . . ."

_____

_____

_____

PRAY

Write a prayer for your friends, asking God to help you to be the kind of friend you want to be to them.

_____

_____

_____

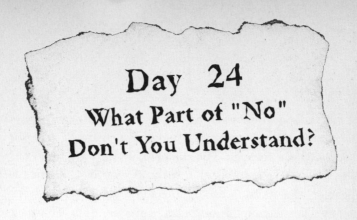

Day 24
What Part of "No" Don't You Understand?

READ: COLOSSIANS 3:1–10

But now you must rid yourselves of all such things as these: anger, rage, malice, slander, and filthy language from your lips (Col. 3:8).

Has a conversation like this ever taken place in your home?

"Dad, may I go to the mall with my friends tonight?"

"No."

"But my homework is done and I—"

"I said no."

"Why?"

"No."

"But . . ."

"What part of 'no' don't you understand?"

Some parents tell their kids no without ever seeming to give an explanation. The result can be a strain in the relationship. The next time you want an explanation from your parents, first go away for a while and cool down. Then return and ask, "Why did you say no?" Yes, it's the same question you always ask, but there is a difference this time. When you asked why before, you were probably a little angry at being turned down. Most of the time, if you ask why with an attitude that says, "I want to understand your perspective," your parents will give you reasons for their decisions.

Here are some ways to get more yes answers. First, save your requests for the kinds of things your parents are most likely to let you do. Second, if possible, bring up the subject several days before you need an answer. This gives them time to think and gives you more time to negotiate. Third, when you do bring it up, present your request in such a way that shows your parents that you have really thought it through. For example, if you want to go on a trip with the youth group over the weekend, but have a major history assignment due on Monday, tell them you will have your work finished by Thursday night—and make sure you do it. Fourth, realize everything depends on timing. Present your request when your parents are most likely to hear what you're saying. The best time may be after a peaceful dinner.

Finally, if they say no, try your best to respond positively. Don't keep hassling them. Just smile and thank them for thinking about it. Also, be prepared for an answer that you might not agree with. You may even think it's a dumb answer. But keep in mind that blowing up in anger will only make things worse. Keep your cool and obey anyway. Your positive attitude will have a positive effect on them, perhaps opening up an opportunity to get answers to your why questions.

My Journal Journey

REFLECT

How does it make you feel when your parents tell you no when you want to hear yes? How do you react toward them?

_____

_____

_____

RESPOND

As you read Colossians 3:1–10, which behaviors described will you begin to change when conflicts arise between you and your parents?

_____

_____

_____

PRAY

"Lord, help my parents and me to understand each other better, especially . . ."

_____

_____

_____

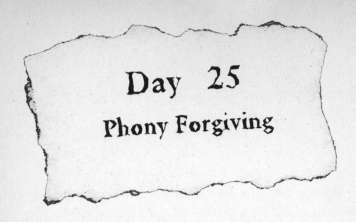

Day 25
Phony Forgiving

READ: EPHESIANS 4:25–32

Be kind and compassionate to one another, forgiving each other, just as in Christ God forgave you (Eph. 4:32).

Giving and receiving forgiveness is the master key to resolving any conflicts you have with people. When you feel offended, you need to forgive the offender. When you are the offender, you need to seek forgiveness from the person you hurt. What is forgiveness? It might help you to see what forgiveness is *not*.

Forgiveness is not just saying, "Well, I'm sorry." When you do that you acknowledge the problem, but not your responsibility for getting yourself off the hook. Forgiveness is saying, "I'm sorry. Will you forgive me?" I also like to specifically state what I am seeking forgiveness for.

Forgiveness is not conditional and cannot be earned. You can't demand that someone change, saying, "Maybe if you clean up your life, I'll forgive you." There are no strings attached to forgiveness.

Forgiveness is not a feeling. There have been times when I sure didn't feel like forgiving someone, and I had to do it by faith. But I can't remember one time of forgiving by faith when the feelings didn't come afterward. Forgiveness is an act of the will.

Forgiveness is not pretending that the situation never happened. So often people just go on with life and act as though there was never a problem. If this is how you are dealing with the situation, don't be surprised when it comes back to haunt you.

Forgiveness does not make the wrong OK. Just because you have resolved your personal hurt through forgiveness doesn't mean that you approve of the wrong done to you or the wrong you have done.

Forgiveness does not mean there won't be consequences. You could still lose your reputation, money, or emotional peace—or face any number of consequences—after a wrong is forgiven. You need to understand that a person who does wrong has a *personal* responsibility and a *legal* responsibility. You can forgive the driver with no insurance who smashed your car, but that person still has to pay the penalty for his or her offense.

Forgiveness does not mean that you won't get hurt in the future. The person you forgive may hurt you again; there is not much you can do to prevent it. But if you forgive now, you will be better able to deal with the conflict and hurts to come.

People hurt each other even in good, healthy relationships. Just because you clash at times with your parents, your siblings, your Christian friends, or your youth leaders doesn't mean these relationships are in trouble. Rather, you can help your relationships to thrive if you are willing to forgive when you are hurt and to seek forgiveness when you hurt others. Two people in a relationship will experience conflict at times, but real love is always ready to forgive.

My Journal Journey

REFLECT

"When I consider the abundant forgiveness God has provided for me, I feel . . ."

_____

_____

_____

RESPOND

After seeing what forgiveness is _not_, how do you need to change your attitudes and actions about forgiveness?

_____

_____

_____

PRAY

"Lord, I want to be kind and compassionate, forgiving as You forgive me. Help me to . . ."

_____

_____

_____

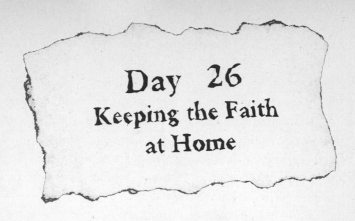

Day 26
Keeping the Faith
at Home

READ: EPHESIANS 6:1–9

*"Honor your father and mother"—which is the first com-
mandment with a promise (Eph. 6:2).*

Nicki became a Christian in the middle of her thirteenth year when a
friend invited her to a youth group bonfire. For the first time in her
life, she felt clean, as though all her troubles were over. When she
arrived home that night, she began to discover that her troubles were
just beginning. She excitedly shared the news of her salvation with her
mom and dad. She expected them to be excited for her. She expected
them to congratulate her. She did *not* expect them to be angry.

"Do you know what time it is?" her father demanded when she
finished her story. "It's after ten o'clock! What did you do all night
at the bonfire?"

Nicki didn't understand. She answered her father's anger with
anger of her own, stomped up to her bedroom, and slammed the
door behind her.

In the weeks and months that followed, Nicki began to grow as
a Christian with the help of her friends in the youth group. She had
never felt as "at home" with anyone as she did when she was with
her Christian friends; nor had she ever felt less "at home" in her
own house with her parents. Nicki's mom and dad showed no interest in her new life. In fact, they seemed determined to thwart her
spiritual growth and church involvement at every turn.

Perhaps you are in a situation like Nicki's. You are a Christian,
but one or both of your parents are not. Or perhaps your parents

are Christians, but other significant adults in your life have not trusted Christ: an older brother or sister, an aunt or uncle, a grandparent. How do you respond to a non-Christian relative?

First, *see yourself as a conqueror, not a victim.* It may be difficult living under the authority of non-Christians, but God can use this situation to build your character.

Second, *see your parents as people, not villains.* They need your understanding and forgiveness, not your criticism and condemnation.

Third, *develop a healthy sense of independence.* While remaining respectful and obedient to non-Christian parents, get involved in other relationships that will nurture your spiritual growth.

Fourth, *make godly choices.* Christ is your complete source of security and significance, so act in ways that are good for you and others and honoring to Him.

Fifth, *be prepared.* Fortify yourself with the truth so you can love, forgive, and accept your parents no matter what their response or your emotions may be.[2]

My Journal Journey

REFLECT

Who are the non-Christian adults in your life, and what impact have they had on your faith?

_____

_____

_____

RESPOND

"I will honor my non-Christian parent(s) (or other significant adults) by . . ."

_____

_____

_____

PRAY

"Lord, help me to find ways to nurture my spiritual growth so I may . . ."

_____

_____

_____

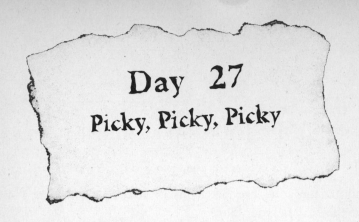

Day 27
Picky, Picky, Picky

READ: 1 PETER 4:8–16

Above all, love each other deeply, because love covers over a multitude of sins (1 Pet. 4:8).

Have you said to yourself, *My parents are hypocrites. They tell me to do one thing and then they do another. It's not fair. Why should I have to do something if they aren't going to do the same?* For example, your dad grounds you for lying and then turns around and tells your mom to say he's not home when someone he doesn't want to talk to calls. Or your parents tell you to go to church regardless of how tired you are, but they sleep in anytime they want. Well, welcome to life.

Few people practice what they preach 100 percent of the time. But that doesn't cancel out the truth of God's Word. He says to obey those over you because of who they are, not because of what they do or don't do. Besides, your parents realize, painfully enough, that they aren't perfect. You don't need to help them to see their faults.

When you are having difficulty getting along with your imperfect parents—or brothers and sisters, friends, or anyone else who sometimes lives by a double standard—remember that love covers our sins. I see so many Christians who feel they have to be the conscience for everybody else. Somehow they think it is spiritual to point out every fault and mistake they see. Paul sets the pattern in Romans 15:1: "We who are strong ought to bear with the failings of the weak and not to please ourselves." So often we try to do the work of the Holy Spirit in dealing with the mistakes of others.

If you truly love people, you will help them carry their weaknesses, not criticize them for being weak. I have met some people whose faith would have been destroyed if I had gone to see a movie. They simply do not believe it is right to go to a movie theater. In that type of situation, it's not right for me to point out someone else's weakness and insist on my right to attend movies. Instead, I spend time with the individual, lovingly sharing where I'm coming from. As I do, it is amazing to see how God brings the person to say, "I can see your point."

Love covers a multitude of sins and carries the weaknesses of others. In Ephesians 4:2, Paul calls it "making allowance for each other's faults because of your love" (NLT). You must be willing to compromise for the good of the other person. Note that this does not apply to moral issues, but to individual differences. In these areas of relationships, love is grace in action.

So when people foul up and you are itching to set them straight, try encouraging them instead. It will work wonders.

MY JOURNAL JOURNEY

REFLECT

What do you sense God is saying to you in today's devotional?

_____

_____

_____

RESPOND

"I believe I can help to improve my relationship with my parents and others by . . ."

_____

_____

_____

PRAY

"Lord, help me to carry the weaknesses of others instead of criticizing, especially . . ."

_____

_____

_____

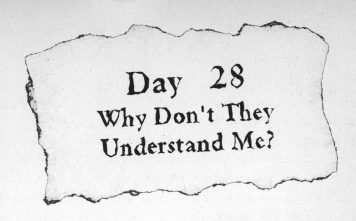

Day 28
Why Don't They Understand Me?

READ: LUKE 2:41–51
*I can do everything through him who gives me strength
(Phil. 4:13).*

So many students have come up to me after meetings and said things like, "Josh, my parents don't understand me. They're always lecturing me, saying stuff like, 'When I was your age . . .' And when they're not lecturing me, they tune me out. What does it take to communicate with them?" Maybe you have felt the same way.

Well, there's good news and bad news here. Let's get the bad news out of the way first. In Luke 2:41–51 you find the story of Jesus at about the time He became a teenager. He and His parents got separated at a big event, and when Joseph and Mary found Him, the young Jesus said, "'Why were you searching for me? . . . Didn't you know I had to be in my Father's house?'" (v. 49). The passage continues, "But they did not understand what he was saying to them. Then he went down to Nazareth with them and was obedient to them. But his mother treasured all these things in her heart" (v. 50–51).

Here's the bad news. If the parents of Jesus didn't understand the young person living in their home, don't be surprised if yours don't understand you sometimes. Remember, your parents grew up in a different era. It is not always easy for them to relate to your generation, but neither was it easy for their parents to relate to them. Every generation struggles to understand the next.

Now for the good news. You can respond to your parents the same way Jesus did, by remaining obedient and respectful in spite of your differences. According to Philippians 4:13, you have the power to do that. Thanks to Christ's strength, it is also possible for you and your parents to grow in your communication skills. Communication is hard work. It is often easier to say nothing than to talk out your differences. Just be careful not to make excuses for not communicating: "They never listen to me anyway"; "We always end up fighting"; or "They just blow me off."

Also, try to avoid responses that choke off communication, like when you

- clam up and say nothing to "get even" for something
- say what they want to hear, then go out and do what you want anyway
- use accusing words like "You never" or "You always"
- keep hassling them until they give in and you get your way.[3]

Don't get frustrated and give up. Keep the lines of communication open. Even though it may feel like you are not making progress, if you try, you really are moving ahead in your relationship.

My Journal Journey

REFLECT

Are you surprised that Jesus' parents did not understand Him?
Write your thoughts and feelings about the story.

_____

_____

_____

RESPOND

"Relying on Christ's strength, I will help to improve communication
with my parents by . . ."

_____

_____

_____

PRAY

"God, help me to remain obedient and respectful to my parents,
especially . . ."

_____

_____

_____

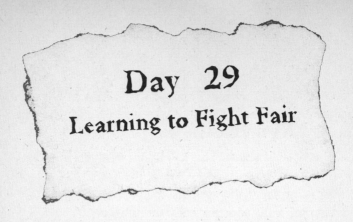

Day 29
Learning to Fight Fair

READ: 1 CORINTHIANS 12:14–27
The eye cannot say to the hand, "I don't need you!" And the head cannot say to the feet, "I don't need you!" (1 Cor. 12:21).

Friendships go through stages. The first stage is the getting-to-know-you stage. During this stage you learn about each other. Then you move to the getting-to-know-you-better stage. This stage holds the potential for the most fun. The third stage is the getting-to-know-you-too-well stage. During this stage you've come to know about each other's bad side. You are tempted to say, "You're too much trouble."

If you haven't experienced any conflict with your best friend, either your best friend is an imaginary friend or you really don't know each other well enough yet. Because when you get to know someone really well, conflict is inevitable. No two people are exactly the same. They have different backgrounds, different perspectives, and different desires. Sooner or later you will have a disagreement. But as you learn to handle your conflicts by "fighting fair," your friendships can grow.

When you have a disagreement with a friend, you have a choice. You can either resolve the conflict or dissolve the relationship. Here are some guidelines for resolving the conflict and keeping the "fight" fair:

1. *Desire openness.* In a fair fight, "I'm always right" is against the rules.

2. *Choose the right timing.* Arguments can break out at awkward times. Wait until both of you have the time and attention necessary to talk things out.

3. *Select the right words.* Think before you speak. In order to know the right words to say, you'll first have to listen to your friend when he or she speaks. Determine if your words will help or hinder in working out the problem.

4. *Look at the other person's point of view.* While your friend talks, listen carefully to understand where he or she coming from. In viewing the conflict, put yourself in your friend's place. When you do this, think of how he or she feels instead of how you feel or why you think your friend was wrong.

5. *Identify the problem.* Discover the main issue that started the fight. It may be more than meets the eye. For example, your friend may have seemed to get upset because you said the wrong thing when actually he or she was already upset because you chose to spend time with another friend.

6. *Determine the solution.* Once you identify the problem, decide on a solution. Make the solution practical and realistic. Don't give up until you have worked things out satisfactorily. Talk about how to keep this conflict from happening again.[4]

My Journal Journey

REFLECT

What are your thoughts and feelings about the statement that conflicts are inevitable when you get to know someone really well?

_____

_____

_____

RESPOND

"In learning how to 'fight fair' in relationships, I most need to remember . . ."

_____

_____

_____

PRAY

Pray through the steps to fighting fair, asking God's specific help at each step.

_____

_____

_____

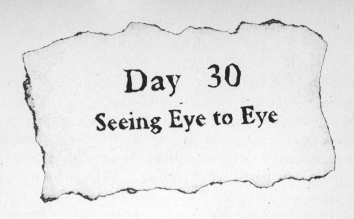

Day 30
Seeing Eye to Eye

READ: MATTHEW 7:1–11

Ask and it will be given to you; seek and you will find; knock and the door will be opened to you (Matt. 7:7).

Here are four great tips from Matthew 7:1–5 for dealing with conflict.

Tip 1: Be humble. Jesus said, "Do not judge, or you too will be judged" (v. 1). It reminds me of the popular saying, "What goes around comes around." Don't be too hard on other people who make mistakes, because you make mistakes too.

Tip 2: Be honest. Verse 3 states, "Why do you look at the speck of sawdust in your brother's eye and pay no attention to the plank in your own eye?" I don't think I have ever been involved in a conflict with someone where I wasn't at least partially at fault.

Tip 3: Practice integrity. "How can you say to your brother, 'Let me take the speck out of your eye,' when all the time there is a plank in your own eye?" (v. 4). Don't blame someone else for your mistake.

Tip 4: Demonstrate love. "First take the plank out of your own eye, and then you will see clearly to remove the speck from your brother's eye" (v. 5). We show love to others by dealing with our own faults before trying to correct theirs.

Here's the danger. You can so easily get wrapped up in wanting to get even that you might miss what God wants you to learn in the situation. The focus should be on finding what God is saying to *you*. This requires a willingness to admit that you are not perfect. Your prayer ought to be, "Lord, give me the strength to own up to my mistakes." Admitting your mistakes is not a sign of weakness. Rather, it takes courage to admit that you are wrong. As you acknowledge the weakness in your own life, you immediately become more able to accept a weakness in someone else's life.

Another important part of learning God's lesson for you is your willingness to be corrected. We can easily be more blind to our own faults than someone else's. A good attitude and a willingness to change are also very important. In every difficult situation between you and the person you're struggling with, you should desire to come out a better son or daughter, a better brother or sister, a better friend, a better employee. Following the four tips above will set the Holy Spirit free to do His work.

My Journal Journey

REFLECT

As you read Matthew 7:1–5, what are your thoughts and feelings about your relationships?

_____

_____

_____

RESPOND

"The tips for dealing with conflicts that I most need to apply today are . . ."

_____

_____

_____

PRAY

Write a prayer to God expressing your heart's desire to work through conflicts instead of trying to get even.

_____

_____

_____

Notes

1. Adapted from Barry St. Claire and William H. Jones, *Love: Making It Last* (San Bernardino, Calif.: Here's Life Publishers, 1988), 88–89.

2. Adapted from Jim Craddock, "Breaking the Cycle: Responding to Your Parents," in Robert S. McGee and Pat Craddock, *Your Parents and You* (Houston: Rapha Publishing , 1990), 166–67.

3. Adapted from William H. Jones, *Parents: Raising Them Properly* (San Bernardino, Calif.: Here's Life Publishers, 1988), 19–20.

4. Adapted from William H. Jones, *Friendships: Making the Best of Them* (San Bernardino, Calif.: Here's Life Publishers, 1989), 45–48.